THE SUCCESS FACTOR

Unconventional
Wisdom for
Small
Business
Success

Ernane Iung

The Success Factor:

Unconventional Wisdom for Small Business Success

Published in New York, New York, by Morgan James Publishing. Morgan James is a trademark of Morgan James, LLC. www.MorganJamesPublishing.com

The Morgan James Speakers Group can bring authors to your live event. For more information or to book an event visit The Morgan James Speakers Group at www.TheMorganJamesSpeakersGroup.com.

ISBN 9781683506171 paperback
ISBN 9781683506188 eBook
Library of Congress Control Number: 2017908979

Cover Design by:
Outside Designer

Interior Design by:
Chris Treccani
www.3dogcreative.net

In an effort to support local communities, raise awareness and funds, Morgan James Publishing donates a percentage of all book sales for the life of each book to Habitat for Humanity Peninsula and Greater Williamsburg.

Get involved today! Visit
www.MorganJamesBuilds.com

Dedication

To my loving wife, Marla, and my daughters, Anais and Ryana. You bring so much joy to my life!

To my parents, Orestes and Maria. I am grateful every day for your unwavering love and support. Thank you.

To my brothers, Orestes Jr. and Silvio. Our fraternity has always been the best brotherhood I have ever found.

TABLE OF CONTENTS

Chapter 6: Referrals: A Little Help from Your Friends 83

Chapter 7: Jack Be Nimble: the Four "P"s of Outsourcing 99

Chapter 8: Virtually Awesome . . . Literally 107

Chapter 9: Cash is King. Don't be a Pawn.   125

Chapter 10: Parting Wisdom   146

Acknowledgements

One of the many nice things about writing your own book is that you can use this particular space to thank as many people as you like, without having to really worry if you're going overboard. Different than say, the Oscars, where winners are oftentimes awkwardly ushered off stage when their thank you's become too long winded. Here, at least, in my own book, I'm guaranteed that I can take the time I need to be as generous with my thanks as I like, the worse thing being you get bored and simply turn the page, thus moving on to the real reason you bought this book. Hopefully, though, I'll hit the mark, thank the people I need to thank, and keep you in tow while doing it.

I first want to thank my wife, Marla Kenia, who is my best friend, partner, and companion. She has patiently let me write and produce this book, and it is the fruits of this patience, love, and kindness which have provided the background for my work.

I would like to next thank my parents, Orestes and Maria Iung. It all begins with them. They have spent a lifetime nurturing, caring, teaching, and showing by example their love for me, first as their son, and today, as a trusted friend. My father, with his kindness, gentleness, and quiet strength, showed me every day what it is to be a man, all the while tempering this with humility and a dedication unique to him and no one else. My mother, in a word, is simply: Mom. After bringing me into this world, she cared for me and continues to care about me, lovingly, unselfishly, unconditionally, and incessantly. She is a model of hope and faith, and I am deeply grateful for the blessing of her life, and the influence she has had on mine.

I would like to thank my colleagues at Liquid Capital Corporation, namely the three founders Brian Birnbaum, Barnet

Gordon, and Sol Roter, but especially Brian who graciously brought me into the company. I would also like to thank Robert Thompson-So, Glen Dalzell, and Steve Buckley, who have mentored me along the road of the fascinating and exciting world of Alternative Financing.

A very special thanks to Paula Hope for her generous contribution on Referral Marketing. Her insights and understanding are second to none, and I am convinced this is an area which will continue to grow in importance, with Paula leading the way through her compelling writing, speaking, and teaching.

Right in the middle of my professional and business thank you's, I would like to thank three individuals who influenced me immensely in high school: Joan Ring, Bob Florkowski, and Paul Dresser. Joan was my absolutely favorite English teacher, and she taught me (and I'm quoting from a handwritten letter she wrote in 1980 that I still have today, where she critiqued my college entrance essay): "The best writing contains the writer. His personality is right there. He makes judgements, positive and negative statements. All else is forgiven if he comes through to the reader." I sincerely hope that I have followed your advice, Joan, and it is me who has come through clearly in this book. Bob encouraged me to have confidence in my intellect and scientific thinking, and has since become a lifelong friend and counselor, not only to me, but also to my family. Paul was the individual who single-handedly got my brothers and me into soccer, and that path has produced a lifetime of wonderful experiences and friendships which could never have happened had it not been for him. A heartfelt thank you to all three of you.

Next, I would like to thank Topher Morrison, who coaxed me into writing this book, but didn't stop there, and has been a consistent friend, ally, and coach throughout the entire process, as well as unselfishly sharing his wisdom and experience as part of my participation in the Key Persons of Influence program. Thanks also to his wonderful staff, especially my fellow Michigander, Jodi McLean, and Sarah Farnan.

Thank you to Alex Rodriguez, who has translated my ideas on style to produce a book that is not only pleasurable to read, but also enjoyable and entertaining visually. I know I have been demanding, Alex, but thank you for your patience. The final product is, in my opinion, brilliant.

Lastly, I would like to personally thank my editors, Brad and Darlyn Kuhn. Your contribution to this book is without measure, and I have so enjoyed working with you, getting to know you, and now calling you friends. Your experience, insights, advice, and patience are deeply appreciated, and I really cannot thank you enough for your outstanding commitment to helping me write this, my first book. Thank you.

Note to Reader

Shortly after I decided to go into business for myself and was in the initial phases of doing a start-up of my own, I began the process of telling a few close friends and family members of my plans. This, of course, included my mother who, after a few moments of quiet consideration, said, "Why don't you apply for a good job at a bank?"

Like many women of her generation, my mother did not have the benefit of pursuing a formal education. That's not to say she's not a sharp lady. Quite the contrary. Seven decades of wisdom from life experiences coupled to her devotion to Bible studies, daily doses of Oprah, Suze Orman, and most recently, Shark Tank, have all helped shape even further her discerning mind.

Mom comes from a generation where people might spend their entire career with the same company. Someone might occasionally inherit a family business, but people in her circles didn't go around starting businesses from scratch. It was risky, she said — like swimming less than an hour after eating a meal. And risk was a bad word in my neighborhood.

I was raised to believe that mothers are always right, so imagine my surprise upon learning she was wrong about post-meal swimming. But mom was absolutely right about start-ups. The Small Business Administration reports that about one-third of businesses with employees fail within two years of start-up, with only half surviving more than five years. With stats like that, why wouldn't you run to the nearest corporate gig that offered a regular paycheck, predictable hours, and benefits?

You have your reasons. And I'm guessing they're a lot like mine. There's something about you that makes you want to run your own show. You have a dream. Maybe it's a new dream, inspired by a new technology or invention; or maybe you've had this dream your whole life and have just been waiting for the right moment to take a leap of faith. You want to bake the world's best cupcakes, craft beautiful furniture out of reclaimed wood, or distribute a perfect new blend of exotic fish food. You'd like to spend your days running the very best Cuban bakery, dry-cleaning shop, landscaping company, cardboard manufacturer, barbecue sauce bottling plant, uniform supply company, or flooring distributorship that your town has ever seen.

You may never achieve the epic success of Google's Sergey Brin and Larry Page, Facebook's Mark Zuckerberg, or Amazon's Jeff Bezos. But who's to say that you won't?

I have a dream as well, and that is to be here for you, as your *Success Factor*, advising, coaching and encouraging you — in print, online, and in person, through my webinars and personal appearances — sharing my lifetime of experiences with you, so that you won't have to take this journey alone.

So be courageous; believe in yourself and your dream; and you will successfully mount a company with a specific product or service that is uniquely and distinctly yours.

Hold on tight. You're in for the ride of your life.

Introduction

If you've picked up this book, you're probably thinking about starting a business, or know someone who is. Maybe you've already started a business and run into some snags that have you thinking about giving up on the dream and going back to work for someone else.

You've come to the right place. I wrote this book for you and people like you, people who really want to make a go of owning their own business, but aren't sure how to go about it. More than anything else, you're afraid of failure. Let me assure you, right here, right now. You've got this. I can help. But first, hand me your brain.

Mm hmm. Just as I thought. The problem is, you're full of it – conventional wisdom, that is.

Conventional wisdom says businesses fail because they run out of cash. (I can fix that, too — helping small businesses with cash flow problems is my specialty.) But a lack of cash is more of an effect than a cause, and I can prove it, with a little unconventional thinking.

As the son of a physician, metaphors relating to medicine are almost second nature. So here's one I know you can relate to.

When a person dies, the blood stops flowing, but most people would agree that the lack of blood flow is a result of the patient being dead, and not the other way around. The blood stops flowing when the heart stops beating, due to a breakdown in some vital organ like the heart or the brain, or a blockage or rupture in a major artery. Cash is the lifeblood of a business. And while failed businesses may run out of cash, the cause of those failures was not the absence of cash, but a flaw in the business model, poor execution, or a cash blockage or rupture caused by slow paying customers or poor cash management. Alternative financing, especially purchase order financing and payment acceleration through accounts receivable factoring, should be part of your business strategy from day one.

So there it is, your first bit of unconventional wisdom (and you're still reading the Introduction!): Businesses don't fail because they lack cash, they lack cash because they have failed.

In this book we address some of the most common failures, most of which boil down to an overreliance on conventional thinking.

Conventional thinking. Being your own boss sounds great, until you realize all of the weight that falls on the boss's shoulders. An owner may not necessarily engage in the physical labor of manufacturing, but all of the other burdens – from deciding what to sell, where and to whom; to the intricate choreography of cash management – are yours to bear. To maximize success, it is important to think unconventionally.

Failed business model. What will you make? Who are your customers? How will you reach them? And how will you get paid? How many people do you need to hire? Who are your competitors? It is important to answer questions like these, and others, in writing, to give your business a structure and a firm foundation.

Bad timeline. Entrepreneurs are notoriously bad at estimating how much cash they'll need to get the company up and running, and how to time expenses to preserve cash and minimize upfront costs. As I will explain in Chapter 3, the timeline for start-up expenditures is everything.

Failure to outsource. Successful entrepreneurs focus their energies on those things that will get the company operational and making money as soon as possible. Owners who try to do everything themselves waste precious time on tactical minutiae.

Conventional wisdom may compel you to do everything yourself. Unconventional wisdom admonishes not to do anything yourself that you can hire someone else to do faster, better, or cheaper.

Ineffective marketing. Successful business owners know their target audience and the best way to reach them. They also understand the value of unconventional channels, such as referrals, online marketing, social media and other digital resources.

Cash drought. Waiting on customers to pay whenever they feel like it is so 20th Century. As I mentioned earlier, payment acceleration, through accounts receivable factoring, or purchase order financing, should be part of your cash flow strategy from day one.

In this book you'll learn to challenge conventional wisdom at every turn. We'll explore the topics above and show you how to build a flexible framework to help you effectively navigate through uncertainty and achieve your business goals.

Along the way, I'll be sharing some of my best business advice. I call them success factors, because they have proven successful for me, in my own business, and have been replicated by of some of the most successful business owners I know.

How To Use This Book

This book is intended to be a fun and quick read that provides a wealth of information to start-up business owners. I'll take you through the first, most important things to consider when starting your company, and contrast conventional wisdom on the topics with the latest, ground-breaking but proven, unconventional wisdom. By the time you finish reading *The Success Factor: Unconventional Wisdom for Small Business Success,* you'll have goals, a timeline, a business model, and a product service offering in place; plus you'll be able to state your value proposition to your market, and how to measure your success.

You'll understand the thinking of your ideal customer, where and how to find them, and how to market in a way that attracts customers you want, while repelling those you don't want. You'll learn to do more of the things you love doing, and less of the things you hate doing. And you'll learn how to get paid faster, and keep more of the money you earn, than you thought possible. Best of all, the success factors and unconventional wisdom you'll learn through the pages of this book are neatly compiled for you at the end, as a ready resource for you to pull off the shelf and refer to anytime you need a refresher.

Learning from Experience, One Another

The first question everyone always asks me when they've learned I've written a book is, "How did you do it?" The answer, surprisingly, is, "It was easy. It came from my heart and my mind, and once I actually sat down to write, the ideas and concepts behind the book flowed naturally. It's a product of 27 years of experiences, working with wonderful individuals and great companies across four continents and more than twenty-five different countries. I absolutely love working with people, and have the philosophy of, in every human interaction, trying to do my best to extract something from that specific experience. I believe we are all teachers and can, through sharing, impart positive lessons on life and work for the betterment of those who choose to pay attention to these shared lessons. I am 'old school' and believe the written word must be elegant and chosen carefully, without abbreviations or short-cuts, and believe vehemently that if we express ourselves in a less rushed, less frenetic fashion, we improve dramatically the quality of our understanding and by consequence, the quality of our business, and business relations. I hope you enjoy your time reading this book and are able to extract learning from my lessons on unconventional wisdom.

It's Time to Rethink
Conventional Wisdom

We are living in the age of innovation, where new technologies outpace our ability to absorb and implement them. Ideas and tools that used to be in the realm of science fiction are at our fingertips, and they are no longer only for the heads of giant corporations. Want to learn how you can harness their power for your start-up?

Ready to rethink? Me too. Turn the page, and let's move on together.

WHAT DO YOU BRING TO THE PARTY?

IN THIS CHAPTER:

1. What do you have?
2. What's everyone else bringing?
3. Bring the good stuff.
4. Function and Framework.
5. Making Money.
6. Multiple Revenue and Equity Discussions

CHAPTER 1

Conventional Wisdom Says:

You can do anything you set your mind to.

Unconventional Wisdom Says:

Play to your strengths, using your natural advantages, and quickly seize the opportunity you have identified, because it may not be around for long.

In graduate school, I played a lot of tennis. Actually, a lot of the students played a lot of tennis where I went to school. When you go to grad school in places like Phoenix, Arizona, the athlete in everyone comes out, and tennis was one of the most popular pastimes for the international crowd at the American Graduate School of International Management. My tennis buddy, Joe, started a hot and heavy romance with a coed named Melody during our first semester, even moving her into his apartment. When their love affair soured early in the second semester, and they split up, Joe threw a party to lift his spirits.

In those days before email and social media, party invitations were scrawled on index cards and thumbtacked to bulletin boards. In addition to the vital details of when and where the party would be held, Joe had written "BYO" — the widely acknowledged acronym for "bring your own" adult libation. None of us grad students could afford to foot the bar bill for all our friends, so BYO was the conventional way things were done, and we'd usually just grab something we already had on hand so we wouldn't have to make a special trip to the store.

Imagine my surprise when I arrived at Joe's place, and saw everyone sitting on the floor. It turns out that when Melody left, she had taken all the furniture. Sizing up the situation, I told Joe, in my usual unconventional way, "Dude, if I'd known BYO meant 'bring your own furniture,' I would have at least brought myself a chair."

A small business is a bit like Joe's party. It's important to ask yourself, "What do you bring to the party?"

What Do You Have?

As a kid growing up in Flint, Michigan, I could never make the claim it was a destination for tourism. Aside from our Brazilian friends and family, it was not a place you would commonly put on your vacation itinerary. Now that I live 10 minutes from Walt Disney World, it's like I'm running a bed and breakfast. When it comes to attracting visitors, sun and fun are natural advantages.

In business, if you are trying to attract tenants for a retail project, it's an advantage to be located near a major highway. If you're a consultant, it helps to have experience in a particular industry. I've started and run a lot of businesses, and I have accumulated a lot of capital. These are my natural assets — the business advantages I already have. That's what I bring to the party. So what do you bring to the party? The list of potential assets is long and varied, depending on your circumstances. A very small business, for example, might have the natural advantage of low overhead. A couple running a lawn maintenance or janitorial company out of their home, could arguably charge less for their services because they don't have any employees or office rent to pay. A farmer might have inherited land. A politician might have a network of rich and powerful friends, and other elected officials who will answer their calls, and trust their judgment as a political consultant.

We're not talking about product differentiation — we'll address that in another chapter. Right now, we're trying to decide what it is you want to do, and the things you've got working to your advantage right from the get-go. For discussion purposes, let's break those advantages down into three categories — Qualifications, Resources, Natural/Comparative.

Qualifications

Having the right talent is critical to the success or failure of your business. Are you naturally creative? Are you good at problem solving? Do people like and respect you? These are natural advantages. More important, however, from a business perspective, is "What have you done?" and because skills requirements change and old contacts go stale, "What have you done lately?" This is the first question a banker is going to ask when you apply for a loan, and considering you are going to be acting as your own banker at first — investing time and money in a start-up — you should ask yourself:

- Do I and my management team have the knowledge, skills

and experience required to run a company?

- Do I/we have a track record of success?

- Are any of us good at sales/business development?

- Is our particular experience/skillset an advantage for a particular type of business?

Resources

Technically this section should be called "Resources Other Than Qualifications, Which We've Already Discussed," but that didn't test well with focus groups, so add that last bit in your head if you need to, and we'll be moving right along.

Like avatars in a massive multiplayer online role-playing game, small business owners accumulate valuable treasures along with the qualifications they gain from experience, resources that might fall into one of three categories:

- **Physical assets** — property, plant, equipment or machinery, tooling, buildings, vehicle fleet, computer hardware; or

- **Relationships** — Personal and Business network, thought leaders, key decision makers, access to distribution channels, customer contacts, and vendors; or

- **Intellectual property** — patents, processes, technology, formulations and training methodologies.

What's Everyone Else Bringing?

I call these kinds of differentiators "natural, or "comparative" advantages — natural because they are the hand you've been dealt and not the result of an intentional marketing initiative; and comparative because they are only an advantage until circumstances change, or someone comes along with an even greater advantage. Business schools apply a stricter definition to comparative advantage, focusing primarily on pricing and efficiency. But I'm not one to let a little thing like tradition muddle my mojo. Stick with me, kid, and you'll go places. Andy Warhol, an icon of the American Pop-Art movement in the mid to late 20th Century, famously foretold of today's celebrity-obsessed society, in 1968, when he said: "In the future, everyone will be world-famous for 15 minutes." Natural advantages are fleeting. Land values change with neighborhood demographics; political advantage shifts with every election; and the half-life of new technology is 18 months and falling. That was the essence of Warhol's "15 minutes of fame" comment. Strike while the iron is hot, because it won't be hot forever.

Bring the Good Stuff

What cards are you holding?

List your skills, starting with those things you are best at. At this point, it is important to ignore any voices in your head that might try to convince you that something is irrelevant. If you're good at it, write it down. Consider this: When Otis Redding recorded (Sitting On) The Dock of the Bay following the Monterrey Pop Festival in 1967, he whistled the outro as a placeholder, intending to replace it with a scat rap, but died in a plane crash before he could fix it. That whistle is one of the things people like best about that song today. Right now, I'd like you to get a pen or pencil, or sit down at your computer or laptop, and answer the following questions:

- What am I best at?

- What do other people think I'm best at?

- What have I done, personally or professionally, that people might pay me to do for them, and why would they hire me instead of someone else?

- Is there anything I've retained from my previous work experience that would help me build my own business?

- What credentials have I earned that would make others consider me an expert?

- What else do I own, or know, that I can use to my advantage in starting a business?

Review your answers. Consider them carefully. Set them aside and come back to them later to see if anything else comes to mind. Now take that piece of paper, fold it, and use it as a bookmark while you read this book. Even if you have already started a business and are just looking for ways to run things better, keep that paper with you. That paper represents the best in you — your greatest natural assets. If you are already making the most of those things in your business, you're on the right track. If you're not, you need to ask yourself why not, and figure out a way to leverage those assets.

Function and Framework

Your business model ultimately determines how your company will profit from the products you make or the services you provide, outlines the mechanics of how you will be paid, and how much money your company will make in a given period. It also sets the stage for three items critical to a company's potential for real growth. I call them the **"bilities."**

The 'bilities are not a backwoods family living remotely in the Ozark Mountains, passing the time angling for catfish, hunting rabbits, and making moonshine. They are three ideas that frame your business model so that it is more robust, flexible, and longstanding. These concepts are scalability, replicability, and sustainability. When choosing the business model for your start-up, ask yourself in what ways it withstands the 'bilities test.

Scalability

Scalability is the ability to ramp your operation up or down, growing or reducing in scale, number, size, or locations. Ease of scalability is a key dimension, as are cost and time relating to scaling the operation. Does it take months and cost a fortune to scale your operation? Or is scaling fast and easy? Obviously, you want a business model that scales easily, quickly and cost-effectively, like a one-piece camping tent with a design that can be set up in two seconds and folded down in five. You get it, camper?

Replicability

Replicability refers to the ease with which you can replicate, or copy your business model. Can you set it up exactly as it is, in its original mode, in various situations, localities, and circumstances, and still run it efficiently? Or is your model so unique that it only functions under certain specific, limited conditions, without which it doesn't operate effectively?

Here, you can see that Scalability and Replicability are closely related. You scale your operation to provide the basic framework to be functional and operational, and then, if you choose, replicate that basic framework in a new region, channel, or with a new partner. By replicating, you are essentially multiplying your basic business model's revenue-generating capability, and in this manner, driving growth. And growth translates to success, and that's what this book is all about, right?

Sustainability

The third 'bility has become a catch word for businesses, and examples of sustainability are everywhere — from coffee growers in Kenya, and silkworm farmers in Brazil, to salmon fisherman in the seas off Alaska. For our purposes, however, sustainability is not of the Joan Baez, environmentalist variety, but a measure of whether your business model can stand the test of time, and still pump out money, which guarantees its continued success.

Time-bound Assumptions Dictate Sustainability

Whenever possible, I try to lock in specific profit margins by product line or service by matching sales contract terms with supply chain pricing characteristics. For example, if the cost of raw materials is fairly stable over, say, a 12-month term, then I would write one-year sales contracts. For example: A 40% gross margin would be sustainable on Styrofoam cups over a 12-month period, due to price stability on benzene feedstock over that period, and a one-year sales contract establishing a purchase price of 15 cents per cup. Longer-term sales contracts might include an inflation clause, or benchmarking adjustment, tied to the cost of goods sold.

Similarly, a service provider might write a contract based on a fixed hourly labor cost, and constant headcount, for the duration of projects lasting less than a year, and add a cost of living adjustment for longer assignment. These time-bound assumptions, which form the structural beams of a sustainable business, are typically expressed in a "business plan," which builds on the foundation of your business model and adds specificity. Generally speaking, a business model defines the way you do business, a business plan defines specific goals and objectives.

The details of how to design a business plan are beyond the scope of this book. In fact, there are entire books devoted to this subject, as well as free and low-cost resources for entrepreneurs online, and if you are interested, would suggest you research this topic further. One last thing about sustainability. As the insurance commercial says, "Life comes at you fast." Your business model must be agile enough to adapt to changing market conditions. In my Styrofoam cup example, I used a planning horizon of one year. Your actual experience will vary according to your product development cycle and supply chain. It is a good idea to periodically test your business model against your business plan, to see if your model will allow you to meet your objectives, or whether additional changes are in order.

Making Money

If your business model has passed the 'bilities test — that is, you've found it to be scalable, replicable, and sustainable, it's time to move on to the central question of, "How do you plan to make money?"

Business models have nuances for each industry or sector. As you dig deeper, you will see that there are also many options and variables of the basic financial model practiced within your industry. With creativity, and a desire to balance the 'bilities with creating a differential for your company's product or service offering, explore the following alternatives within the money-making dimension of your business model. Let's start with the basics:

1. **How will you bill?** By the hour, by the project, by retainer, by charging monthly or annual fees, or even usage fees?

2. **How will you collect?** Will partial fees be due up front, or is payment in full due at order placement, or upon delivery?

3. **Will you offer credit?** If you finance your customers' purchases, what are the terms, credit limits, and default

rates commonly practiced in your industry and market?

4. **What are the standard payment terms?** Are they 30-60-90 days (i.e. retailers, corporate clients, and insurance companies), requiring you to wait for payment while you make payments to your labor force, payroll taxes, and fixed and material costs every week?

5. **Based on industry research, how many of your customers are likely to be "slow payers"?** Ten percent? Twenty-five percent or more? If most or all of your customers pay at an average of 45 days out, where will you get the cash flow to survive?

6. **What's the profile of your labor force?** Will you use full- or part-time employees, or work with freelance professionals for flexibility to scale your workforce up or down, depending on the volume of projects in the pipeline?

Let's look at some different businesses to see how their business models affect day-to-day operations and cash flow.

Multiple Revenue & Equity Discussions

Let's touch upon two of the more innovative options that you may want to consider, at least partially, as potential business models for your newly minted company. The first involves creating multiple revenue streams for your business, and the second is the "money for equity" model that has been made famous by reality shows like ABC's "Shark Tank" and CNBC's "West Texas Investors Club." Both programs showcase the business model of entrepreneurs pitching business ideas in exchange for investment, equity, and ultimately, access to the business acumen that made the millionaires on each show famous (although one does it with 3-piece suits, and the other with cheap cigars and Miller Lite beer).

Multiple Revenues are Easy — Honest

When considering alternative business models for your business, the question is not how you can make money but rather, how many ways can you make money? And that speaks directly to developing multiple revenue sources as an add-on to your basic business model. Let's say you're Abe Limon, and you've just launched "Honest Abe's not so famous Ale" craft beer, designed and brewed in Baton Rouge, Louisiana. You've signed a few local distribution agreements with several beer distributors and sales are chugging along. Life, beer, and business, in general, are good. But through your efforts on social media, you've noticed your beer sells particularly well in markets where there are large groups of actors and entertainers, who have somehow identified with your "not so famous" logo, because in reality, they all want to be (famous, that is).

So in markets like Las Vegas, with its casino entertainers; New York and Chicago, with their Broadway shows; and L.A., because of Hollywood, your beer sales are booming. So how to drive more business, in addition to the direct sales through your normal channels?

You leverage options presented by the multiple revenue source model. Here are a few suggestions from Honest Abe's example:

1. Licensing local brewing in the markets of Nevada, Illinois, New York, and California, obtaining royalties on sales plus the licensing fees to the craft brewers of "Honest Abe's not so famous Ale" in each new state where it is now being brewed.

2. Explore selling over the internet on sites such as "The Beer Connect," which sells craft beers online.

3. Develop export sales to Canada and Mexico as a result

of the connection of your licensed brewers in New York and California.

4. Is this idea capable of being a franchise? (Meaning can it be replicated easily in any number of geographic locations over, and over again?)

5. You have connections with high level people in the airports in some of your key markets, and you get a license to set-up a "Beer Kiosk" in the airports of the cities where you have established local brewing. Sales are not huge, but the marketing for "Honest Abe's not so famous Ale" is priceless, and as a result, Abe's Ale is no longer not so famous.

So now, instead of one, traditional revenue source for your business, you now potentially have five additional revenue sources, which could include:

1. Licensing fees based on beer production volumes

2. Royalties on sales from your licensed brewers

3. Sales commission on Internet sales

4. Export sales revenues to two international markets

5. Kiosk sales revenues

Obviously, this is a hypothetical example, but it shows you that with a little creativity, you can add one, two, three, or more new revenue streams to your core business model, and in this way, drive growth, make more money, and create a buffer against downturns in your traditional sales channels.

We have Sharks in Texas, too

The basic premise of the two successful reality shows, "Shark

Tank" and "West Texas Investors Club" relies on entrepreneurs giving up an equity stake in their company in exchange for financing that is needed to further grow the business — financing needed to buy raw materials, complete a prototype, scale the operation, enter a major retail channel, or any number of other options. Sound familiar?

As an alternative to conventional bank financing, the Shark Tank model offers start-ups or small businesses direct investment in exchange for equity in the company. Additional services which may be offered by the equity firm could also include:

1. Access to select distribution channels

2. Financial management

3. Tax planning

4. Marketing services

5. Partnerships

6. Preparation for an initial public offering (IPO) or sale

How do you value an equity investment? Every situation and company is different, and the actual valuation will depend on the combination of sales history, management expertise, company assets, intellectual property, technology, etc. But in general, an estimation of the short-term annual sales of a company is made, and the equity stake is a percentage of that investment. For example:

Honest Abe's not so famous Ale is currently doing $500,000 in annual sales. But after securing online beer sales contracts and an export sales contract, plus kiosk sales for Chicago O'Hare and the John Wayne airports, you are now projecting annual sales at $1.2 million. There's a catch, though. Honest Abe needs capital to ramp up production to meet the online and export sales figures, and kiosks cost $3000 each, and you'll need 20 (or $60,000) just to start your business in all the terminals of these two airports. Total estimate for your new business development needs is $400,000 — money that you don't have.

If you can substantiate a new sales level of $1.2 million, then a $400,000 investment will represent a 33 percent equity stake in your company. Today, at the $500,000 sales level, the 33 percent stake is worth $167,000.

If Abe gets to $1.2 million, it will be worth the original investment amount of $400,000. And if it grows successfully to, say, $5 million, the 33 percent investment will turn $400,000 into $1.65 million, for a 312.5 percent increase in investment.

That's how the equity game plays out, and how the Sharks make (or don't make) their money.

So the "Shark Tank," or investment in exchange for equity, business model is an attractive one, but requires that a business owner have a viable and already lucrative business (which you may not yet have) as well as requiring the business owner to give up some control of the company. Whether this is a good or bad situation for the business owner depends on the owner and the partner he or she chooses. With risk there is reward, but nothing is as straightforward as it seems on TV, and although attractive, this model is certainly a tricky one.

Lastly, in this model, if it is successful, and at the end of say, five years, the owner and their equity partner can sell the business, the returns can potentially be even higher. In the Millennial world we live in, this model may be as good as any, given the uncertainty of things due to the unprecedented speed of change and obsolescence. Here the motto of: "invest, build, grow, and sell" may be the smartest unconventional wisdom I can offer you on this option.

Chapter 1 Success Factors

1. Make a list of your natural assets/advantages.

2. Determine whether any of those assets will give you an advantage over competitors.

3. Make sure you are putting your natural advantages to their highest and best use.

4. Build your "'bilities."

5. Quantify how much money you'll make, how long you'll wait to get paid, and how you're going to bridge any critical gaps.

READY.
AIM. FIRE!

IN THIS CHAPTER:

1. Ready – The power of goals.
2. Aim – Plan for the unpredictable.
3. Fire – Go the distance.
4. Reload - Plan for growth.

Conventional Wisdom Says:

There is a magic formula for success.

Unconventional Wisdom Says:

The path to success is unpredictable, so set clear goals, plan for uncertainty, and go the distance.

There's a funny story from the 1950s about the law of unintended consequences, in which Marilyn Monroe proposes to Albert Einstein, saying, "With your brains and my beauty, think what children we could have." Einstein replies, "But what if they have my looks and your brains?"

Start-ups are like that. Much of what you expect doesn't pan out, and much of what happens, you didn't foresee. Faulty thinking and failure to properly account for uncertainty are two of the primary reasons why businesses fail – according to QuickBooks, a popular small business accounting, payroll and payments software and business platform. To succeed, you need clear goals, a business plan flexible enough to accommodate uncertainty, and the ability to execute that plan effectively.

It's easy to visualize this in archery terms. First, we set up a target (Goals), then we take all known variables into account (Aim), and then we execute the plan (Fire). As the plan is executed, we measure the outcomes, take aim, and fire again. In this chapter we explore this iterative process before taking you step-by-step, in subsequent chapters, through the critical decisions in starting a business, all viewed through the lens of unconventional wisdom.

READY – The Power of Goals

There's a name for a business without goals; it's called a hobby. Nothing wrong with hobbies; they're just not businesses. If you are reading this book, I have to assume that you mean business. And before you can conduct business, you have to get READY. That means setting written goals.

Goals are powerful. They have their own gravity, which pulls you toward them. This is important because the business environment is dynamic. With so many variables in motion, goals provide a focus and establish a benchmark against which outcomes can be measured.

AIM – Plan for the Unpredictable

A lot can happen between the time an arrow leaves the bow and arrives at the target. A strong headwind can cause it to fall short, a tailwind can help it along, and a disruptive crosswind can deflect it wide of the mark. Businesses face headwinds, tailwinds and crosswinds all the time. Here are some examples:

- A product line you expect to sell well doesn't (headwind), but another one, surprisingly, does (tailwind).

- The sales channel you expected to enter easily doesn't present itself (crosswind), but another one, unexpectedly, does "headwind".

- Your business plan counts on sales to a large retail customer that doesn't pan out "headwind", but several smaller ones appear in its place "crosswind".

- Your new high-powered saleswoman with great industry experience and an impressive contact list doesn't produce "headwind", so you end up making the most of the team you have "tailwind".

- Your bank says "no" to your credit line request, alleging new regulatory restrictions "crosswind", and you've already tapped out personal savings, credit cards, and family members "headwind".

If you start with the premise that you absolutely must plan for unpredictability, and build a business model that allows for a variety of potential outcomes, you will insulate your start-up from the perils of the unexpected. Risk managers do this all the time through scenario planning. They call it "credible challenge." By challenging your own assumptions, you protect your downside, and put your company in a position to pursue upside opportunities as they present themselves.

A colleague once expressed his business model as, "Two 'ifs', and I'm out." Any deal that included two or more variables beyond his control was off-limits for him. Thinking unconventionally, I would suggest that a more realistic model for start-ups is "All 'ifs', and I'm still in, but I'm going to proceed with caution."

So how do we take this notion of planning for the unpredictable and bring it to Earth so that it has real impact on helping your start-up succeed? The following exercise takes you through the top-level scenario planning logic of a hypothetical distributor trying to gain its first contract with a national retailer.

Business goals:

1. Enter a large mass retailer in the first six months of operation

2. Certify two SKUs from a third-party manufacturer

3. Use a credit line provided by a local bank

Alternative scenarios:

GOAL 1

Variance: Open three smaller, regional retailers.

Predicted result: Reduction in projected first-year sales, but improved cash flow and profit margin attributable to better payment terms and larger profit margin.

GOAL 2

Variance: Certify only one SKU from your manufacturer.

Predicted result: Lower marketing and promotional spend, resulting in savings to sales, general, and administrative expenses.

GOAL 3

Variance: Bank declines credit line request.

Predicted result: Explore additional financing options — invoice factoring, purchase order financing, and equipment leasing, through a cash flow specialist, such as Liquid Capital.

Scenario planning "brackets" a range of possibilities, from "best case," to "worst case," on either side of the expected outcome, eliminating guesswork, and allowing the company to shift smoothly into alternative actions in a revised plan. You, the business owner, must formulate the three or four premises unique to your business, and then, based on these, **plan for the unpredictable.**

FIRE – Go the Distance by Executing Your Plan in Detail

Conventional wisdom focuses on the importance of having a good plan. Unconventional wisdom recognizes that even the best plan isn't worth the paper it's printed on unless management – in this case, YOU, can successfully navigate the headwinds, tailwinds and crosswinds to hit the target and achieve the goal.

Whether you are talking about the nail-biting pre-launch phase of your business, where cash flows are all expenses, or later, when large cash outlays or slow-paying customers threaten to create temporary cash droughts, your success depends on your ability to execute.

Elite endurance athletes have a winning strategy that involves getting out ahead of the pack by setting a pace that will deliver a winning time, conserving resources to go the distance, and saving any big "kick" or sprint until later in the race, when it is absolutely necessary.

Applied to the pre-launch phase of a start-up, that strategy looks something like this:

1. **Set a good pace** – The first goal is to get through launch and reverse the cash flow from negative to positive as fast as possible. The longer it takes to start invoicing, the harder you'll have to work to break even.

2. **Control the timeline** – Carefully plan the key elements of your timeline to ensure that your starting capital lasts until your company starts generating money.

3. **Minimize the maximum** – Limit pre-launch payments to essentials, and postpone your largest pre-launch expenses – like rent, payroll, equipment, and training – as long as possible.

The same strategy can be adapted to project management and post-launch cash management, although there are additional options I will discuss in Chapter 9.

RELOAD - Plan for Growth

There's an old Brazilian adage, "Be careful not to step longer than the length of your legs," that warns against the dangers of reaching too far, too soon. If you take on a project or accept a new order, but falter on delivery, you risk ruining your reputation, or even taking down your company.

Conventional wisdom might interpret that to mean, "Grow slow." Unconventional wisdom says that by building growth into your business model (scalability), you lay the foundation for success. Here are three ways to do that:

1. **Location, location, location** — Being in the right place at the right time is one of the smartest decisions you can ever make for your company. So, choose wisely. Whether you are trying to pick a fast-growing market — as I did when I selected Orlando after a nationwide search — or a particular hot spot within that market, do your homework. Some cities and states are more business-friendly than others. Research the economy, growth rate, infrastructure, comparative wage levels, business climate, taxes, development incentives, and competition. When picking a specific site, check traffic patterns, crime rates, housing

starts, pedestrian traffic, seasonal business trends, and business failure rates. Generate several options, research them online, and then visit them in person.

2. **Ownership structure** — Your ownership structure will shape the course of your relationships with financiers, customers, and suppliers. Options include: Sole proprietorship, Partnership, Limited Liability Company (LLC), or Corporation. Each have their own unique characteristics and advantages — sole proprietorships are easiest to form; corporations provide the best liability protection and are the most flexible when it comes to adding and subtracting owners/investors. With your attorney and tax professional, choose a legal entity structure flexible enough that it allows you to grow into it or along with it, not one that will require changes at each step, costing you valuable time and money.

3. **Risk management** — It may or may not be true that "if you protect the downside, the upside will take care of itself," but the more you grow, the more you'll have to lose. Check into risk mitigation strategies like liability insurance (both general and business-specific). Other insurance, such as life, health, disability, and business interruption can be crucial, as well. Ask yourself what would happen if you or your partners couldn't do your jobs for any significant length of time. What would happen to your clients, your customers, your family, and your assets? Protect them and yourself from the unpredictable. Research any regulatory requirements for your industry and establish a proper framework of governance and controls. These days you also have to think about your digital downside. Protect your valuable data by identifying your "crown jewels" and making sure that you and any vendors with access to credit card or other confidential data comply with all data

security laws.

Be optimistic. Look beyond where you are, and include in your small company plan or start-up a plan for growth.

Chapter 2 Success Factors

1. **READY** – Focus intensely on your basic start-up goals: i) get operational, ii) start the clock, and iii) control the timeline.

2. **AIM** – Plan for the unpredictable using a detailed, highly flexible business plan.

3. **FIRE** – Execute effectively by keeping your goals in mind and conserving resources to "go the distance."

4. **RELOAD** - Plan for growth from the get-go.

TIME IS (NOT) ON YOUR SIDE

IN THIS CHAPTER:

1. The Timeline is Everything.
2. Make Bread, You Need Dough.
3. Hold onto Your Dough 'til You're Ready to Roll.
4. Timeline Essentials – The 5 Ps

CHAPTER 3

Conventional Wisdom Says:

"Timing is everything," suggesting that anyone who comes up with the right idea at the right time can't help but succeed.

Unconventional Wisdom Says:

The timeline is everything. Hold onto your starting capital as long as possible. Carefully time your launch expenses and manage your operating cash flow to avoid putting yourself behind the eight ball before you've even banked your first revenue.

With money in the bank and a good start on a career in advertising, 20-year-old Walter had it made. But Walter didn't see himself as an ad man. He had an idea for his own company — a cutting edge tech start-up. His timing was perfect. He was entering the business in the earliest stages, a time when fortunes are made.

Walter worked nights and weekends developing his prototype and doing a little market research before going all in — leasing an office; buying equipment; and hiring a salesman, a business manager, and four techs. It took all the money he had, but his timing was right. And timing is everything, right?

A big order came in from New York. The team worked without pay, as Walter deftly dodged the landlord, knowing that a big payday was just around the corner, and that the end would justify the means. They finished the work and shipped it by deadline, but the customer never paid. The start-up failed and Walter lost everything.

Conventional wisdom failed Walter, but he did gain some valuable experience. And experience taught him that while timing might be important, it's the timeline for cash flow and expenditures that counts when it comes to sustaining a business through startup.

Cash timing is something you're going to read a lot about in this book. In part, because I'm in the cash flow business. But also because, like the music in musical chairs, when the money stops, the game's over.

The Timeline is Everything

I cannot emphasize this enough: The longer it takes to get your company up and running, the longer the odds you'll succeed. Why? Because once you build the infrastructure of your company, hire the people, and establish the physical work environment; the longer it takes to start selling, the more you consume — instead of produce — the most basic commodity of your operation – cash.

One of the most important questions to ask and answer when developing your start-up's launch timeline is, "How long will it take for the company to not only generate its first income, but actually receive its first cash?" I am constantly amazed by how many business owners fail to consider this question, or if they do consider it, severely underestimate the time it takes. They then wonder why they are out of cash.

Here's an example of what can happen:

To Make Bread, You Need Dough

My client, a frozen bread manufacturing start-up, was outfitted, staffed, and ready to roll, when she got some bad news. Turns out she had neglected to obtain several certifications from state and federal regulators. To make matters worse, an Occupational Safety and Health Administration (OSHA) pre-launch inspection report demanded several worker-safety improvements, some requiring local zoning approval. Although none of these were serious violations, they all had to be addressed before she could open, and by the time she was able to get everything addressed to OSHA's satisfaction, her launch date was pushed back 7 months.

Imagine the expenses: 7 months of salary, 7 months of cold storage refrigeration, a fully-staffed plant just sitting there, idle. After 7 months without the factory producing a single loaf, investors began to apply pressure, demanding to know when they could hope to see any kind of return on their investment. Although I empathized with my client, I understood where her investors were coming from.

This situation could have been avoided, or at least minimized, with a timeline in the business-planning phase. Critical tollgates related to certification and zoning requirements, rather than the hiring process, should have driven the timeline. The operation was now looking at a break-even date that would take several years, rather than several months, to accomplish, all as a result of inadequate planning.

Hold On To Your Dough 'til You're Ready to Roll

The success factor missing from my client's plan was a detailed timeline forecasting cash expenditures to the exact day, if possible, and delaying the actual check writing to the last possible moment. Once the check is written, there is a cash outflow, and the only way to get that money back is through sales. If your sales timeline is too far in the distant future, you may be digging a big hole for yourself.

Walter, from the beginning of the chapter, could have used a timeline as well. But here's some good news. Eventually Walter realized that cash flow timing was not his gift – an insight that bankers were, no doubt, glad to share the next time he tried to start a business.

Fortunately Walter had a brother who understood the importance of careful cash flow timing. And once Walter teamed with his brother Roy, the Disneys were well on their way to success.

Timeline Essentials — The 5 "P"s

To craft a good timeline, you need to get your Ps (but not your Qs) in order. Below I have laid out the essentials, what I call the "Five Ps" of a good timeline.

1. **Place** —The first order of business is to establish the location where you will be conducting your business. This will be the point, even if initially it's only a mailbox,

where all your correspondence for your start-up or small business will go. It is this address you will list on your papers of incorporation, your 'Doing Business As' (DBA) if you plan to use one, tax documents filed with the IRS, business cards, and marketing collateral. For a physical location, where you will be interacting with customers, you should conduct traffic studies; analyze zip codes for the concentration of potential customers in a defined geographic radius; do competitor analyses; and evaluate the municipalities or states which offer your business the most optimal tax benefits, incentives, or exemptions for establishing your business in that particular location.

2. **Permission** — There is no shortage of 'permissions' a small business owner must obtain before the business can commence operations — USDA licenses, sales and use tax certificates, business licenses, zoning permits, trademark filings, licenses from the Alcohol and Tobacco Tax and Trade Bureau ("TTB"), fire permits, air & water pollution control permits, wholesaler's licenses, distributor agreements, and merchandising licenses, to name a few. Why are "permissions, processes, certifications, and licenses" the second item on your timeline essentials and not somewhere in the middle? Because they are beyond your control, and they will generally involve slow, prickly bureaucratic organizations which, depending on who you are (or aren't) and what state or municipality you are dealing with, can drag the process out without much regard to your individual timing or needs. This important, but often overlooked, step can add months to your timeline, so you want to make sure you get this out of the way before you hire employees or take on other overhead that will add to your break-even or payback period before you start conducting business and making money.

3. **Payability** — To get paid, you need a payment system. Whether that system is an online system like Quickbooks, or an elaborate enterprise resource planning (ERP) platform, you will need time to select, install and train on how to create and send invoices, and how to record payments. This is a critical piece of infrastructure, and you would be dead in the water without it. Be sure to include a "Plan B," to prevent business interruptions due to systems glitches. This should go without saying, but I have worked at a major global enterprise that had to scramble to "rent" ERP capabilities from an accounting firm, because they didn't plan for contingencies. This is a good example of where it pays to "plan for the unpredictable," as I mentioned in Chapter 2.

4. **Product** — Product fulfillment is a key metric of most retail situations, and suppliers or vendors are measured not only on the sales and margins they generate, but also how well they deliver those sales. Your customers are going to judge you based on your ability to deliver specified quantities, at the time and date requested. One thing you don't want to happen is for orders to start coming in for which you don't have product to deliver. You need to establish and plan for a clear course to sales; either through purchase orders issued, firm letters of intent, or distributor agreements; or have a product that you know, once you put it out, essentially sells itself. Every business is different, and the customers are calling the shots. Some may require a month's inventory, others 15 days' worth, and others may stretch you to 2-2 ½ months of inventory.

5. **People** — Conventional wisdom says get your people first, because a company is only as good as its people. But unconventional wisdom says hire them last. Normally

people and companies get so revved up about their business they just can't wait to tell people about it and jump the gun to get key people onboard. This is an expensive error. Employees are likes kids — once you have them, you've got to throw all kinds of money at them. Kids need clothes, food, books, toys, vacations, and want to eat at McDonald's (or Mackey Doughnuts, as my 4-year calls it) every week. Employees are the same. Do you know what the one thing a good employee loves to do more than anything else? Show you how good they are. They want to show and prove to you what a great, value-adding employee they are. They show this to you by wanting to go out and visit customers, take them to lunch, go to trade shows, network at pricey luncheons, and do a million other things that cost money. It is much better for you, as the newly minted small business, to bring employees on last. I know that sounds counterintuitive, but don't fall into that trap. You won't need employees until you've taken care of the other four Ps on your timeline. That's the unconventional wisdom that assures you start out on the right foot and ultimately helps guarantee your short- and medium-term success.

There actually is a sixth timeline essential, but it's not a "P", it's an "F," and that's Financing. And, if you haven't figured it out by now, when I say financing, I'm talking about alternative financing. Conventional wisdom says to use bank financing as the principle source of funding of your start-up or small business venture. Unconventional wisdom states that alternative financing, or in the case of this book, factoring and purchase order financing, should not be an afterthought to your financing regimen, but rather, should be considered as your primary source of funding from Day 1. This is one of the most important premises of this book. I'll be coming back to it frequently, and I've got a whole chapter on the subject at the end of the book.

Chapter 3 Success Factors

1. Build a detailed, in-depth timeline as a central piece of the business plan.

2. Go from being a consumer, to a producer, of cash as quickly as you can.

3. Time large initial expenditures as close as possible to your first influx of cash from sales.

4. Take care of the 5 Ps of a perfect timeline: Place, Permission, Payability, Product, and People.

WHO
NEEDS IT?

IN THIS CHAPTER:

1. Solve a problem.
2. Differentiate.
3. Build it where your competitors are not.
4. Swim upstream.
5. Just look inside.

CHAPTER 4

Conventional Wisdom Says:

"If you build it, they will come."

Unconventional Wisdom Says:

Define your ideal customer. Make their lives better. And do it better than anyone else.

There is no shortage of product and service offerings out there; according to the U.S. Department of Agriculture there were almost 40,000 new consumer packaged goods items launched in 2016 alone. That, despite the fact that the average grocery store stocks only about 40,000 items, and the average consumer is a creature of habit who buys maybe 260 different products in a year — or less than 1 percent of available product choices. And that's just one sector of business.

Think about it. That bed you woke up in, those pajamas you tossed in the hamper — the hamper itself — that shampoo you washed your hair with, and that cereal bar you ate for breakfast, your toothpaste, deodorant, mascara and eye liner were all products. And I'd be willing to bet you've been buying those exact same products for years. What would it take to get you to switch — especially to a new product neither you, nor your friends, has ever heard of? There's no way to know without asking. And it's way too risky to just guess — although too many do just that.

Getting people to switch products or services is hard, especially for a start-up. An easier approach might be to focus on identifying a problem people are trying to solve, and crafting a solution that solves it better, or at least cheaper, than anything else on the market

Solve a Problem

Very generally, I'm now going to walk you through a simple rationale to assist you in crafting your product or service offering for your new business or start-up. Some of it may already be familiar to you, or it may be altogether new to you. But follow me, using a tool which I feel is the most effective, which employs the Problem Solving Method. This straightforward rationale will provide you clear answers on which to base your offering and, at the same time, generate the building block components of your economic model.

The first step, then, in the process of crafting your product or service offering, is to ask yourself what problem you are trying to solve. Talk to people who have that problem — or, alternatively Google "Consumer Product Research" and you'll find a long list of companies with established networks of volunteers willing to participate in consumer surveys. These companies offer great analytics and understand how to help you design probing questions for optimal and actionable results. Next, determine who has that problem and how widespread the problem is. The old joke is: Don't try to sell ice to Eskimos, but I'm also pretty sure people visiting Disney World's Magic Kingdom would do just about anything for a decent meal while passing the day at the U.S.'s favorite theme park (sorry Walt).

Third, find out whether the people with the problem can afford to buy your product or service. You can build the best mousetrap in the world, but if the citizens of Hamlin gave all their money last month to the Pied Piper, you'll need to look elsewhere for customers.

Fourth, ask yourself if your customer and the end-user of the product or service are one and the same. You might sell your product to a distributor or an original equipment manufacturer (OEM), instead of to the person who ultimately uses it. When you brush your teeth tonight, ask yourself if you bought that paste from the lab that developed the cavity-fighting, tooth-whitening formula; the factory that pumped it into the clever little flex-tube; the truck driver who delivered it halfway across the country; or the megastore where you also bought milk and paper towels.

Fifth, do market research to determine if the aspect of the product or service that excites you is the same as the value it will bring to the customer. Are you delivering value based on cost, technology, quality, or service? What combination of those categories does your customer care most about? For a smartphone, it might be technology; for a massage therapist, service. When buying a new car, does the customer care more about cost, or quality? Different demographics will produce different answers. Know the demographic for which you are solving a problem.

Differentiate

What is unique about your product or service? What would make your ideal customer choose it over your competitor's line? What are the trends in your industry, and what are you doing, instead of copying your competitors, to make sure that you offer a better experience? How can you differentiate, and be compellingly different?

Creating value doesn't always mean offering the highest possible quality at the lowest possible price; it means finding that optimal combination of price and quality that makes it impossible for your customer to even consider going to your competitor instead. So how do you do this? Through differentiation. What do I mean by that? Let me give you an example you can easily relate to: Jimmy John's Gourmet Sandwiches.

What's the difference between Jimmy John's, Subway, and Firehouse Subs? Only one, Jimmy John's, delivers. And not only do they deliver, they do it at break-neck speed. You've hardly hung up the phone and the little Jimmy John guy (or gal) in their 2008 Silver Toyota Corolla with the JJ sign magnetized to the car roof, is at your door, with the engine running; and they're already asking, "Mind if I keep the change?"

Jimmy John's lightning-fast delivery service is a clear differentiator, because as much as I love Subway and Firehouse, there are times where I don't feel that I can break away from my work to go out and grab a bite for lunch. And it's those moments where I reach out and call my trusted friend, Jimmy John, because I know my 8"-inch Pepe sub will be delivered fresh to my door before I've even scrounged out the change to pay for it.

Similarly, why would people choose my company, Liquid Capital, over another alternative lender? At Liquid Capital we differentiate ourselves with perhaps the alternative financing industry's largest product selection — a range which begins with traditional products like factoring of accounts receivable and purchase order financing, and extends all the way to more sophisticated operations like asset based lending (ABL), import/ export financing, and revenue based lending. Our biggest competitor, Bibby Financial, offers primarily factoring and ABL products, while Liquid Capital, on the other hand, goes well beyond that. We also position ourselves as having the industry's best and most robust back-office services, with U.S. operations consolidated in our Dallas, Texas office, and Canadian operations in Toronto and Montreal.

What makes you different? How are you unique in your city, region, state, sector, or industry? When you look at your competitors, what is the one or even two things that set you apart from them? Remember it doesn't have to be 100 different things. If chosen correctly and carefully, it can be as simple as that single dissatisfaction present in your industry or sector that you are able to solve. More examples: is it product, like with me at Liquid Capital? Is it cost? Is it delivery, like Jimmy John's? Is it packaging? Whatever it is for you, find a way to articulate and communicate it in everything you do, and this will become the clear differentiator of your businesses product or service offering. It's that easy.

Build it Where Your Competitors Are Not

My Liquid Capital operation is in Orlando, Florida. Heard of it? It's home to not one, but seven theme parks, the U.S.'s second largest convention center (first is in Las Vegas), 24,000 timeshare properties, 87,000 hotel rooms, a population of roughly 262K and growing (2014 Census), with per capita income of $27,069 (2015) and growing. Florida also ranks high in a study performed by the Tax Foundation, due primarily to the fact that it does not have a state income tax. (By contrast, California's state tax is 13.3% of income.) Additionally, to help companies avoid additional corporate income tax, Florida exempts "S" corporations from state taxation. So it's just not sun, beaches, Miami Vice, and Disney that draw people to Florida, but also the robust and attractive economic environment for businesses and start-ups.

Coming back to the unconventional wisdom of "build it where they are not," I recommend strongly and emphatically that you consider going to a state, city, or municipality that offers the best incentives on taxes, business start-ups, job creation, employment to vets, whatever, that you can find. Do your homework (recall my advice on research earlier in the chapter), and don't settle on setting up your business in Lazytown just because you are from there.

If you bought this book, you are no doubt driven and aspire to make your business a success, and success involves many tough decisions and sacrifices, the first of which may involve moving to a new place, away from where you are today, but which offers you and your business a competitive advantage in terms of taxes, exemptions, territory, or wages. I'm not endorsing any one particular place, but if you have a commodity business which is highly price-sensitive, you may want to consider one of several states, in addition to Florida, which do not have a state income tax — Texas, Washington, New Hampshire, South Dakota, Wyoming, and Montana. It may not seem much now, but if you can scale your business, following the advice laid out in Chapter 1, say to $5 million annually, a 6% sales tax equates to $300,000. And that's a lot of money, by anyone's standard.

It is well known that football is a game of inches. Business, likewise, is a game of percentages — where 1% can make the difference between being a small business success, or another statistic for the Small Business Association on business failures. So make your business decision to "go where they are not," because you got into this business for it to succeed, and if moving to a new state or location is what it takes, then the decision should be an easy one.

Swim Upstream

As an endurance swimmer, participating in aquatic marathons for over 10 years now, I've found that there are two good strategies you can adopt at the start of each race. If you are fast, confident, and can swim with the big boys, you take your position in the front. The idea here is to try to get out fast, away from the kicking, pulling melee that generally characterizes the start of an open water race. This is the tactic I use. I always position myself at the front — because I'm old enough and cocky enough to want to swim with guys half my age — that's part of the reason I even do it!

The alternative tactic, used by my friend and fellow endurance athlete, Thomas Mantz, President of Feeding Tampa Bay, involves positioning yourself at the back of the pack at the starting line. Here, you wait for the line of swimmers to move forward, gradually entering the water, and you simply follow the flow while the others trip and kick themselves silly. Both approaches employ a premise analogous to our next piece of unconventional wisdom, which states that if you look around and it's crowded, separate yourself from the crowd. In an aquatic marathon, you do this by positioning yourself at the front or rear of the pack. In business, you do this by going upstream, the equivalent of adding more value to your basic product or service offering.

If during the process of designing your product/service offering you find that you are intensely competing in the same space as many of the other companies or brands which are offering nearly the same product or service, shift your focus upstream. In this way, you create differentiation by adding more value to your product or service offering. This is a spin-off of the basic model of differentiation, but differs in that it requires that you differentiate by adding value, rather than by being different.

What do I mean by this? Let's say that you make and sell designer Belgian chocolates. You're competing against a whole lot of folks — some with very powerful brand names like Godiva and Rococo. To get away from merely the comparison based on chocolate and the design of your truffles, you customize the individual wrapping of each truffle and the exterior of the box. Packaging is expensive, but for that customer who really wants something special and unique, your concept is a winner.

Or, say you make craft beer. This is a red-hot market with literally thousands of microbreweries springing up from São Paulo, Brazil to Macomb, Georgia. How do you set yourself apart? You could date stamp each bottle and can, to assure customers they are holding the freshest suds their money can buy. Date stamping requires rigorous control of production lot size, distribution, and sale, but you're adding value (a guarantee of freshness) that you believe sets you apart from the artisan brew crowd.

There are two basic things to keep in mind when designing any upstream strategy. The first involves controlling the cost of the added value — you don't want to price your product or service out of the segment in which you are competing. And the second relates to assuring that your upstream differentiator is perceived by your targeted customer. Your customers have to perceive that there is added value in what you are offering as a differential. If you do these two things, then your decision to follow unconventional wisdom by swimming upstream when your market or industry gets overly crowded should put you at the top of the podium at race end.

Look Inside

What is unique about your product or service? What would make your ideal customer choose it over your competitor's line? Sometimes the answer can be found by just looking internally at your own company. The last method I am going to discuss on alternatives for deciding on the best product or service offering for your new business involves simply looking inwardly toward your own company, its employees, and their special skill sets.

- Do you have particular areas of expertise? For example, do you have a lot of experience in particular markets, such as working with corporate lawyers, consumer durables, plastics, or graphic design?

- Do you have unique knowledge of a specific geographical area or social class (i.e., Hispanic, Asian, or Indian) that could set you apart?

- Do you have unique relationships or knowledge in dealing with government contracts that could provide you a leg up on other companies providing the same service?

These factors and more could help you establish a particularly attractive product or service offering that is unique to your company, just because you looked inside and discovered that someone or some group within your own company had developed an expertise or differential that now makes your business unique.

Chapter 4 Success Factors

1. Ask what problems your proposed product or service solves. Do the research on problem solving before you invest in a product or service offering.

2. Determine what your end users need that you could provide.

3. Differentiate to create a winning value proposition for your product or service.

4. Avoid crowds, and establish your business in a city, municipality, state, or country which provides you and your business a competitive advantage.

5. When the competitive landscape gets too crowded, do like an aquatic marathoner and distance yourself from the crowd; but in business, do it by going upstream.

6. Find the optimal combination of price and quality that makes it impossible for your customer to even consider going to your competitor instead.

7. Consistently review whether the experience of the ultimate user of your product or service could be improved

EVERYTHING YOU ALWAYS WANTED TO KNOW ABOUT CUSTOMERS

IN THIS CHAPTER:

CHAPTER 5

Conventional Wisdom Says:

Cast a wide net to catch and keep as many customers as possible.

Unconventional Wisdom Says:

A few well-chosen customers, with whom you enjoy working, are worth more than many who make your life miserable.

I have worked with many wonderful customers during my long career and in my travels. In nearly every case I have come away with invaluable lessons. Every customer had a story to tell. Each had a unique style. Some were great at arbitrage (buying low and selling high). Others were brilliant marketers, working their brands, promotions, and store formats to create unique retail experiences that captivated their own customers, ensuring loyalty and repeat business. And then there were the operations managers, measuring and calculating everything, from the time customers spent in the store, to average sales prices, repeat buys, and warehousing dollars per square foot.

My point is that not all customers are created equal. For every customer you love, and who loves you back, there are many you'd frankly be better off letting go. How can you tell the difference? That's a skill it took me years to master. Even now, I'd be lying if I told you I always get it right. I am, however, much better than I used to be. Customer relationship management is worth an entire book of its own — and there are many available. I'll do my best, in the next few pages, to give you a condensed version of what I've learned in my more than 25 years of deal-making. This is probably one of the most important lessons you'll ever learn.

A New Spin on the Old Win/Win

One thing all customers have in common, every single one, is that when it comes to negotiations, they all want to win. Talking about finding a win/win is all good and fine, until you actually sit down at a negotiating table. I've been both the big dog and the little dog at that table, and I can tell you, the big dog always eats first.

I don't say that to rain on anyone's parade. But people are essentially self-interested. And most clients don't give a fig for what you want out of the deal. The extent to which they get their way is largely a function of how big they are, and how much you want/need their business. It's nothing personal. Some of my toughest clients are some of my closest friends. It's just a matter of leverage. You'll find that leverage often applies on the backend as well, because larger customers — especially the operations types, can be some of the slowest to pay, and the least flexible when it comes to accommodating expedited payment requests.

It's Not About You

No story sums up the reality of customer/supplier relationships better, in my mind, than the story of Alex and Eric.

Alex was an accomplished sales manager, having been promoted through the ranks from small accounts to regional manager and finally to key accounts supervisor. He was likable, credible, and a very good negotiator. The problem was, his biggest customer was, well, bigger.

Eric was the son of a Polish-American who'd escaped the Nazis to establish one of America's largest value retail chains. The family-owned business had over 500 stores, a huge advertising budget, and a media presence that made it a household name.

The company grew so large that Eric's father had brought him and his brother into the business. The brother he put in charge of sales and marketing. Eric landed in charge of purchasing and finance — a Chief Financial Officer (CFO) before that title came into vogue.

Just prior to the close of every month, Alex and Eric would enter into negotiations for the next month's orders — a form of mental torture that always left Alex feeling sick and mentally drained. He'd hold out as long as he could. But his company needed the business, and Eric knew it. So Alex would always end up capitulating, giving up precious margin at the expense of his own company.

After one particularly difficult negotiation, as Alex was toting up the losses in his head, Eric patted him on the shoulder and offered him a drink. "I'm really happy with the deal we've just completed," he said. "You see, at the end of the day, it has to be good for both of us."

"Good for both of us?" Alex asked in astonishment.

"Yeah, for both of us," said Eric. "Me, and my Dad."

Manage Expectations

Small business owners spend so much time thinking about their customers, it's easy to see why they might think their customers are also concerned about them. As my story illustrates, they really aren't.

Customers, in general, have one priority — their own business. And to be honest the same is true of the small business owners, who only think of their customers from a business development and sustainability perspective.

Customers know that suppliers and service providers are important components of their success, and they may even remain loyal as long as they are getting sufficient value out of the relationship. At no time, however, would they consider the needs and wants of vendors over their own self-interest. The companies that supply them with goods and services are not their priority, and never will be.

The sooner you realize, as the owner of a small or start-up business, that to the customer, it's not about you, the better it will be for your business. By paying attention to this cold, hard fact, you'll avoid the illusion that your customer is interested in promoting your company and your brand, or in facilitating the growth and profitability of your company. They're not, and that's not bad; it just means you should never let yourself become too dependent on any one customer.

Like assets in an investment portfolio, the more diverse your customer base, the more stable your business will be.

Be Careful What You Wish For

In December 2003, Charles Fishman, a senior writer at Fast Company, wrote an article detailing how mega-retailer Wal-Mart's relentless performance pressure on its suppliers had forced some companies to lay off workers, send jobs overseas, and sometimes even close up shop. Fishman used the example of Huffy Bicycle Company in what he calls the "damned-if-you-do, damned-if-you-don't Wal-Mart squeeze."

During the 1980s, Huffy sold twenty styles of bikes to the retailer at varying price points and profit margins. One style was an entry-level bike priced at a thin profit margin, and Huffy committed to supply as many as Wal-Mart needed. Sales took off, and Huffy faced a demand for 900,000 bikes, versus their capacity to produce only 450,000. Huffy knew the retailer's reputation for demanding its suppliers do what they say they will do. So in order to free up production capacity to make the cheap bikes for Wal-Mart, it gave designs for four of its higher-quality, higher-margin bikes to rival manufacturers to fulfill.

Huffy lost money in three of the five years before Fishman's article ran, and made its last bike in the United States in 1999. China, Mexico, and Taiwan now make the bicycles Americans ride.

Although both Wal-Mart and Huffy insist that the Wal-Mart relationship did not force Huffy's hand, the story does serve as a cautionary tale to small business owners who may dream of "striking it right" by signing a distribution deal with a major retailer. Because what you gain in sales volume, you could very well lose in margins, resulting in a situation where you are working far harder, for less profit, and so dependent upon the volume that you give away any negotiating power.

Unconventional wisdom states that a customer relationship is only good as long as it's good for you. The moment you detect falling, or deteriorating margins, debilitating cash flow due to unfavorable payment terms or working capital strains due to unusually high inventory stocking requirements, you must reassess the situation. That will most certainly require a renegotiation of the terms of the sale. If you cannot improve on the key components of the deal so that they are more favorable to you, you must be prepared to cut bait and walk away. Otherwise, you are putting at risk everything you have worked so hard to build. And the question becomes, "Is selling to this one customer worth risking the livelihood of my operation?" Unconventional wisdom states that not all customers are created equal and the answer here is, "No."

Defining the Ideal Customer

Baseball catcher, manager, and coach "Yogi" Berra kept America in stitches with his quotes that, at first blush, seemed nonsensical; but upon reflection, were quite wise. My favorite is, "Baseball is ninety percent mental. The other half is physical."

While it may have been mathematically challenged, Berra's quote is particularly applicable to business start-ups. Ninety percent of everything you do relates to customers. The other half is everything else.

Your customers are at the heart of everything you do, or should be. They are not only the reason your company exists, they are also primarily responsible for its success or failure. So choose your customers wisely.

Wait a moment. Don't the customers choose you? Of course they do. But if you manage a few things correctly, you can be sure that the RIGHT customers choose you. You may be thinking that, as a start-up, you should be grateful for any customer who wants to work with you. Who has the discipline to turn away business? People who've wasted time and energy working for the wrong customers, that's who. Experience teaches us that having to work with the wrong customers can be worse than having no customers at all.

So how do we know or predict whether a short-term "dream" customer over time will evolve into a nightmare? You start by understanding your customer's problem.

Choose Wisely

The first step in ensuring you find the right customers is to understand the problems your company can solve, which you've already done using the method we discussed in Chapter 4. Once you have a good idea what those problems and solutions are, you can start to figure out who is most likely to suffer from those problems. Those people/companies are your prospective customers.

Next, articulate why you and your company are uniquely qualified to solve the problems for your customers. This means digging deeper into the problem, by asking yourself to whom the problems your company can solve would be most troublesome. Who would have the most to lose by not dealing with these problems? If you can demonstrate to those folks that the cost of NOT sorting out the problems would be GREATER than the cost of dealing with them, then your case becomes compelling. The more a client needs your products or services, the better your negotiating position.

Remember your natural advantages? Do you have a particular area of expertise? Do you have experience working in particular markets? Do you have unique knowledge of a specific geographical area? Are you better at getting on with certain types of people? All these factors can help you narrow your focus and establish an attractive offering.

Consider aspects like emotional upheaval, stress, and the risk to the customer's reputation, when implementing your solutions to their problems, as well as a bottom-line cost. All these factors comprise the value in your offering.

Also be able to articulate why you and your company are uniquely qualified to solve the problems for your customers. This means doing research on the competition.

Define the Customer

Now that you know what the problems are; you're confident your company can solve them; and you've determined what groups of people are most likely to suffer from the problems, you are ready to paint a detailed portrait of your ideal customer. This is one of the first things I did, when I opened my Liquid Capital franchise. This is how it's done:

- Take your list of potential customers who suffer from the problems your company solves, and group them by location. For example, high-net-worth individuals tend to live in certain postal codes. Group them by market sector, such as manufacturers, recruitment agents, service providers, retailers, etc.

- Ask yourself relevant questions about the prospects on your list. Are they married or single? Male or female? Baby boomers, Millennials, Empty Nesters? What is their level of education: post-graduate, college, or none? Define them in as many relevant ways as possible.

What type of potential customer profile is starting to float to the top? Each of these groups will create a potential segment for you to target further. Are they writers, athletes, or entrepreneurs? Do they live and work in certain geographical locations? A big city, the seashore, farm country? Are they members of certain specific market sectors? Manufacturers, accountants, technicians?

Today we live in a world of niche marketing. Whether you want to work with cattle growers in America's heartland, technicians from a large eastern city, or West-coast athletes; the worldwide web is a fantastic venue for connecting with customers who need personalized products and services, cutting out many distribution challenges that previously existed.

By concentrating on a specific customer profile, particular

industry or market segment, you will know which websites to view, which publications to read (and possibly write for), what associations to belong to, and which networks to join. Within a narrow and well-defined market, it will be easy to become well-known. Without limiting your market, it will be difficult to know where to even start.

Criteria for Ideal Customers

My friend and mentor, Topher Morrison, Managing Director at Key Person of Influence USA, in Tampa, Florida suggests using two simple criteria for business owners who are developing their ideal customers. Ask yourself, first, "who do you like"? His advice here is to select as customers people with whom you really enjoy working. And second, "who has the money"? He is convinced it makes no sense, no matter how much you like them, to develop a business model around people who haven't the money to pay for your products or services.

"You don't want to work with somebody that you don't like who has a lot of money, or with somebody you like who doesn't have any money," Topher says. "Find that happy balance of **people you enjoy working with, who also have money.**"

By the way, if your warning bells are going off that you should turn down a customer, pay attention to your instincts. Those bells are there for a reason. If you've lived a long time, you know, instinctively when a relationship is not a good fit. And if a customer is not a good fit, they won't be happy; you won't be happy; you'll be wasting your time; and you'll be miserable.

I know what you're thinking: You need customers. Shouldn't you work with anybody who wants to work with you? Not many new business owners have the self-discipline to turn down business. I didn't, until Topher taught me the art of segmentation.

Segment Your Target Market

Many marketing and communications agencies will offer to create a website for your start-up that will appeal to everyone, and will make them think you're speaking directly to them. They will urge you not to alienate anyone, since you don't know who will visit your website and want to work with you. That is absolutely the wrong approach when starting a business.

If you try to be all things to all people, you'll end up being nothing to anyone. You have to figure out for whom you can create a truly unique, remarkable product; from whom you will then receive the largest amount of revenue in the shortest possible timeframe. Today it's all about finding people you have things in common with. This ideal customer is your Avatar.

So, going back to your prospecting methods, determine what people you have things in common with, what people you like, and make sure they have enough money to buy your product or service, and develop your communication strategy so that it attracts ONLY those types of people. This may sound strange, but you actually want to repel the audience you don't want within the first few seconds they come across your marketing message. If your message isn't clear enough to do that, it won't be clear enough to attract the ones you do want to work with.

Reflect on the following celebrity spokespeople: Martha Stewart. Rush Limbaugh. Oprah Winfrey. Howard Stern. Jerry Springer. Rachel Maddow. Admit it. You either love each one or hate them. There is no middle ground. Their powerful brands repel people who don't have the same belief systems, and are extremely attractive to those that do. Consider their examples when creating a marketing plan for your small business or start-up.

Speak to Their Needs

If you are not speaking to the needs of your Avatar, you're certainly going to have a much lower close ratio than if you are speaking to your ideal customer. But if you qualify appropriately each prospective customer along the way, by the time you are in a face-to-face sales discussion, you can template your pitch to include the same points, to ask the same questions, and predict the same responses, because you are essentially speaking to the same type of person, every time.

Topher's company uses a system called the 'type' form. By the time the client is in the office for a sales conversation, they have filled out the form and have been segmented into A, B, C, D, or E leads. The company is so busy talking to qualified As and Bs, they no longer even book appointments with the Cs, Ds, or Es.

Prospect questionnaires are available online from various sites and many are industry specific. You program as many questions as you like, and they can be in your preferred format — yes or no, multiple choice, or even essay. The purpose of the questions are to determine how closely the prospect matches the qualities of your Avatar, and also to determine if they are experiencing the top three problems of your target audience — the very same problems you identified using the methods outlined in the previous section, which your product or service has been crafted to solve.

Once your prospect knows that you understand what their specific problems are, and that you empathize, you will forge an emotional connection or bond, that will have them nodding 'yes, yes, yes,' during the sales conversation, and clamoring to sign a sales or service contract right away.

A Final Word about Customers

If you are not having fun and working with the people or groups you enjoy, then why go through all the effort? One of the surest ways to guarantee you will enjoy your work is to make sure you target those groups, segments, or industry sectors for which you have passion, and to which you offer value. So when it comes to customers, do your homework, listen to your heart, and work with those whom you enjoy. That's the unconventional wisdom.

Chapter 5 Success Factors

1. Always negotiate with awareness that customers are in it for themselves.

2. Customers will use suppliers and service providers as leverage to satisfy their end consumers.

3. Don't let your business evolve to overwhelming dependence on one particular customer.

4. Understand the problems your company will solve for the customer.

5. Demonstrate that the cost of NOT solving problems is greater than the cost of solving them.

6. Paint a complete, detailed picture of your ideal customer.

7. Look for customers you enjoy working with, who also have money.

8. Develop a communication strategy that repels the people you don't want to work with, and attracts those you do want to work with.

REFERRALS: A LITTLE HELP FROM YOUR FRIENDS

IN THIS CHAPTER:

CHAPTER 6

Conventional Wisdom Says:

Business owners must be well schooled in myriad marketing methods – advertising, telemarketing, direct mail, POS marketing, pipeline development, conversion, satisfaction, and retention, to name a few.

Unconventional Wisdom Says:

Marketing, while important, varies by industry, product, and service offerings; but relationships developed and nurtured from focused efforts in referral marketing, are the key drivers and success factors for a small-to-medium sized business and its customers.

The information in this section was graciously contributed by Paula Hope, co-author with Susan Crossman of *"Your Personal Marketing Playbook."* I am extremely grateful for her input and expertise, as well as her friendship, coaching, and mentoring. And as I walk you through the unconventional wisdom of a platform built on Referral Marketing, I know you will be too.

Here's what Paula says about finding customers through referral marketing:

Referral Marketing

Referral Marketing is a very young term for a very old method of creating revenue. In fact, it was the original method of creating new business. Imagine John the caveman saying to Peter, another caveman, "George, the man who makes spears in our village, is the best around! Go to see him for your weapon." John created a referral by sharing his trust in George with Peter.

The most overlooked method for growing a start-up business is referral marketing. It is best defined as the systematic cultivation of business by referral, and it is the business world's best-kept secret. It's the system by which business owners create, manage, and leverage their social capital to generate referrals.   Its origins are founded in the concept of "word of mouth," the passing on of a message from one person to another. Referral marketing is about creating a plan that capitalizes on word of mouth to generate referrals. It starts with networking and ends in strong referrals that catapult business owners to stratospheric levels.

Invest in Social Capital

Put another way: the most effective, authentic and powerful method of growing your business will be you. This concept of personal marketing is about creating, managing, and leveraging your social capital. In Paula's new book, *Your Personal Marketing Playbook*, she defines social capital as the goodwill that you create with members of your network. That goodwill starts with giving, helping, and developing trust with members of your network.

Why is social capital so important to personal marketing, and really to everything you do? Because, on or offline, the reception of your message depends entirely on the social capital that you have created with the member of your network who is being approached. They will be motivated or demotivated to respond to you according to the relationship that you have established with them. The simple truth is that social capital is the building block of all relationships, and relationships are the key to all social interactions. And to your start-up success.

Cultivate Trust

Relationships, and most certainly the strong relationships that create referrals, do not happen overnight, and in most people's worlds, strong relationships do not occur often enough. Your role is to develop deep business relationships of trust and confidence in you because a referral is a transfer of trust. That's right. Referrals cannot happen unless trust is present. Trust is the hallmark of a strong relationship and a good referral.

Never insult a referral by calling it a lead. A lead is an idea, where no trust has yet been transferred. Please do not settle only for leads from your network. You want beautiful referrals. When you combine a relationship that has trust, along with deep knowledge of your business, plus confidence in you, plus referral marketing knowledge, you will receive very well-qualified, easily closable, beautiful referrals.

By continually tapping into your network for referrals, you will grow and grow your start-up business to maturity. But is referral marketing all about getting? Of course not. The more you give to your network, the more business development opportunities you will receive.

Be a Giver

One of the most important concepts of Paula's referral marketing platform focuses on the concept of giving. As a Christian, son, father, husband, and business professional, I have been able to identify deeply with the merits of this method. Long before referral marketing was in vogue, the Bible taught us to "Give, and it will be given to you. A good measure, pressed down, shaken together and running over, will be poured into your lap. For with the measure you use, it will be measured to you." **(Luke 6:38)**. Also, in **Acts 20:35**, the Apostle Luke writes, "I have showed you all things, how that so laboring ye ought to support the weak, and to remember the words of the Lord Jesus, how he said, 'It is more blessed to give than to receive.'"

So although we are talking about the application of Referral Marketing in a business context, the act of giving has been present since the beginning of mankind and is abundantly present and discussed in the Bible and through the teachings of Jesus Christ. What I want to say here, is that call it what you like, referral marketing or just plain "giving" has a well proven context for our very existence since the beginning of time.

Paula writes further that referral marketing is based on the "law of reciprocity". If you give to a person who is also a "giver," they will do everything they can to return the favor - in time. While it is important to give for the sake of giving, and not hold your network member accountable for immediate reciprocation (else, you will not a "giver be"), a natural outcome of your generosity is that your network member will want to help you.

Dr. Ivan Misner and Michelle Donovan summarize this point in The 29% Solution: "By giving to others first, you take the initial step in building two-way, win-win networking relationships. You're being proactive and positive. You're leading by example, modeling the behavior you hope others will adopt".

Now, the first concern of all givers is, "How am I going to give to members of my network? I would have done so before I understood that giving was such an important business strategy." The answer to this question is easy and comes naturally to many of us: Listen.

Listen

The answer lies in the two biggest assets that you have - your ears, of course! Listen - just listen – and do it actively. And ask good questions. Find out more about your valued networker's business goals. Make sure that you understand the real benefits, or actual takeaways, to their customers - and that you can repeat those benefits clearly to other members of your network.

The other tactic for your two biggest assets, your ears, is to listen very carefully when people talk about their problems. When members of your network are inconvenienced by a business, household, or personal problem, and they share these issues with you, think of other members of your network for whom these complaints may be moments of opportunity.

Ask yourself who you know who is:

1. **A business problem-solver:** a coach, lawyer, trainer, accountant, consultant or any other business service

provider who might be able to help with this challenge?

2. **A household problem-solver:** an organizer, decorator, painter, senior's specialist, contractor or any other home service provider who might be able to assist?

3. **A personal problem-solver:** a psychologist, fitness trainer, nutritionist, skin care specialist or any other personal care provider who may be able to help?

In the process of giving referrals, you will, at the same time, be expanding your referral trust network, because individuals will be receiving referrals from you — without having had to ask for them directly from you. And that is the beauty of the method of referral marketing. You give, others receive, trust is transferred, and problems are solved. It's a perfect circle.

It Must be Measurable, Too

Just because it is based on the age-old process of word-of-mouth, doesn't mean that referral marketing is devoid of important metrics. At Liquid Capital, Paula has us use a measure called the "Booked Solid Scorecard" which is a weekly tool for measuring our referral activities. I have adapted this into **The Success Factor Referral Matrix**® and I'll explain how it works below.

The Success Factor Referral Matrix® breaks your referral activities down into five primary areas called "Tactics." Each tactic and its description is detailed as follows:

1. **One-on-One:** Refer to meetings or encounters you have individually, with persons in your network to tell them about yourself and your business. Here your aim is to build trust, or possibly have them make referrals on your behalf to generate revenue for you and maybe even themselves, if you have a formal, signed referral agreement with them.

2. **Face-to-Face:** This is where you go out and give "face time". It's usually in groups where you may be volunteering at charity or fund raising events, sponsoring some form of activity, working with a network member on an activity of theirs, or participating at a trade show where you are circulating, making contacts, purchasing, or even just blowing your own horn.

3. **Online:** This is self-explanatory and is anything and everything you do online – for my Millennial readers, this is likely the activity you may do best or feel most comfortable with in the realm of referral marketing. Here I'm referring to updating your profile on LinkedIn, tweeting on Twitter, blogging, posting, commenting and liking on

your social media of preference. There is a newsletter activity in this book, which may involve adding a network member to your newsletter, as well as an important activity related to your website which can include calls to action, lead generation, and demand or content generation. THIS IS SOMETHING YOU SHOULD DO EVERY DAY.

4. **Pure Referral:** I call this tactic "Pure Referral" because it is referral marketing in its purest sense: giving. Here you are giving unselfishly and generously to members in your network by providing referrals, arranging meetings or speaking engagements, sending articles of interest, calling on network members simply to connect, nominating members for positions or jobs, and so on. Investments made here pay big dividends in the future.

5. **Events:** What are your networking groups? Here you track and measure your participation in the events of the networking groups where you are active. (Paula Hope suggests that you have at least 3 network groups in which you participate.)

You will see that each activity has a "Point Weighting," or a value assigned to it. For each time you do that activity during the week, you enter it underneath the column of the day of the week. *The Success Factor* **Referral Matrix**® looks like the following:

The Success Factor Referral Matrix®

Week & Date	Week 3, March 20-24, 2017
Tactic	**Activity**
One-on One	In-depth meeting with network member.
One-on One	In-depth meeting with Referral base member.
Face to Face	Volunteering, Recruiting, Researching, investigating.
Face to Face	Advising, Announcing, Shopping Around.
Face to Face	Trade Shows: Purchasing, Connecting, Inviting, blowing your horn.
Face to Face	Collaborating with a network member
Online	Maintenance of your online presence (updates, likes, additions)
Online	Your Web site activity - call to action, lead & content generation
Online	Blogging, Posting, Commenting
Online	Inviting, Recognizing, Horn Blowing, Sponsoring
Online	Newsletter - mailings, content sharing, contact management
Pure Referral	Giving a referral to a member of your network
Pure Referral	Arranging a meeting or speaking engagement for a network member
Pure Referral	Written testimonial for a network member or referral
Pure Referral	Phone call to network member to simply to connect with them
Pure Referral	Sending article of interest to network member
Pure Referral	Nominating a network member
Events	Networking event (breakfast, lunch, Happy Hour, Panel discussion)
Events	Personal activity with at least 4 people you coordinate (wine tasting, golf, etc.)

The Success Factor Referral Matrix®

Point weight	Mon	Tues	Wed	Thurs	Fri	TOTAL
5	-	-	-	-	1.00	5.00
10	-	1.00	-	1.00	-	20.00
5	-	-	-	-	1.00	5.00
5	-	-	-	-	-	-
5	-	-	-	-	-	-
10	-	-	1.00	1.00	-	20.00
3	1.00	1.00	1.00	1.00	1.00	15.00
3	-	-	-	-	-	-
3	-	1.00	-	-	-	3.00
3	-	-	-	-	1.00	3.00
3	1.00	1.00	1.00	1.00	1.00	15.00
10	-	-	-	-	1.00	10.00
10	-	-	-	-	-	-
5	-	-	-	-	-	-
5	-	2.00	1.00	1.00	-	20.00
5	-	-	-	-	-	-
5	1.00	-	-	-	-	5.00
10	-	1.00	-	-	-	10.00
20	-	-	-	-	-	-
Total	3.00	7.00	4.00	5.00	6.00	131.00

Each activity has a weight, and totals to the right-hand column. Your objective EACH WEEK, as you build your referral network, is to total at least 120 points per week. Track your score weekly and then average your weekly score for a monthly point total. Again, the magic number is 120 points, and you must maintain at least this average number on a monthly basis to guarantee you are building your referral network adequately.

Over time, you will see trends that show areas where you are strong, or maybe weak. For instance, if you are a Millennial, you are likely to score well in the "Online" tactic section, but less on the "One-on-One" section. The personal meetings are fundamental to establishing the transfer of trust so important to referral marketing, so you will see quickly if it is an area where you may need to dedicate more time. Likewise, you may also see that in one particular month you participated in very few networking events. In the next month, in the spirit of continuous improvement, you know to focus and plan to participate in more networking events, be it breakfast meetings, happy hour, spring social, or whatever is happening on the calendar of your networking groups.

Invest in Yourself

Let's be clear on one thing: this is a big investment for you. It will be a different experience from any other new business development method that you will have ever experienced, including cold calls, walk-ins, or public relations campaigns. The good news is that your referral marketing journey will require a much smaller financial investment upfront than any other new business development method. At the same time, the bigger part of your investment will be in time, focus and, yes, heart.

Expect a lot of personal growth from your investment in referral marketing. You will cultivate many parts of yourself as you grow your network, cultivate your Referral "A" team, and develop the programs of mutual benefit on which you and your team collaborate together. And the results from these personal investments are going to be exponential.

Beneficial Outcomes

And lastly, to prove to you its power, consider these proven statistics on the outcomes from your investment in referral marketing:

1. **The closing rate (the percentage of referred prospects which result in a closed deal) is a whopping 34%.**

    Yes, one in three referrals, where an average amount of trust is transferred, ends up in a deal. Imagine what happens to the closing rate when there is a really high level of trust? The closing rate goes up to 80%! With this level of referrals, almost every time you receive a referral, it will end up in a close. That really high level of trust is created by you and your referral marketing knowledge.

2. **Your confidence is much higher when you approach a referred prospect.**

    The likelihood of your closing an exceptional deal will be higher when you meet a referred prospect, because of your own confidence. Many referred business owners have remarked on this feeling. Trust in you has been transferred to you. You already share a respected member of your network with your prospect. You will have your best game-face on. Remember: praise your referral source enthusiastically (a key referral marketing strategy).

3. **Price is less of an issue with a referred prospect.**

    Have you ever been in a meeting with a referred prospect

when the meeting has gone so well that price becomes less of a concern for the prospect due to the relationship that you have with the referral source? It always amazes me that concern about price can be so quickly diminished by trust that has been transferred. Trust = Value. TRUST = $$$$. Very powerful!

4. **There is often an adoption of additional services during the first year of business.**

    There are statistics to support the fact that referred prospects are more open to the addition of additional services from a referred vendor within the first year of the business relationship. Interesting. The trust platform from the referral continues to resonate powerfully during the first year, and onward.

5. **There is the creation of a referral culture within the new relationship.**

    A referral culture has been modeled by you and your referral source. Even more referrals occur in a relationship that has evolved from a successful referral.

So, the reasons for investing in referral marketing abound!

Your Personal Marketing Playbook Bonus

One last key point about integrating referral marketing into your world:

In any organization, all hands should be on deck to assist with new client development, including and especially, the executive levels. How many accountants, lawyers, or consultants achieve partner level without bringing a considerable number of new and high-quality clients along with them to their new lofty heights?

And yet, there are many business professionals who want to hire a sales professional to handle new business development for them as soon as they can afford them. The best (and, for some, the worst) news? You are always the best sales person for your company, if you understand and embrace the power of personal marketing.

To summarize Paula Hope's generous contribution to your new business knowledge, I would like to add the following:

Implicit to referral marketing is the act of unselfishly giving to your network and its members. Without expecting reciprocity, you give referrals, recommendations, suggestions, endorsements, and connections. Your radar is constantly set on exploring ways to help your network, proactively thinking about their needs and their businesses. The best way to grow your market is by giving.

Through my experience at Liquid Capital, I've learned that when you give to members of your network, it may not come back to you directly from the specific members who received your endorsements, recommendations, or connections, but it WILL come back to you from the network at large. Now that's what I call unconventional.

You can learn more about Paula and her other books by visiting **www.bookedsolid.ca.**

Help Customers to Find You

In addition to seeking customers through referrals, it's important to make sure that people outside your referral network, those who haven't heard of you, nor you them, but that fit your ideal customer profile perfectly, can find you. Chapter 8, on building a search-engine optimized mobile/digital media strategy, will help make that happen.

Chapter 6 Success Factors

1. Relationships are the key to obtaining and retaining customers.

2. Define your customer in order to choose your specific market.

3. Unselfishly giving to your referral network is the way to grow your market.

4. Measure and track your Social Capital activities using *The Success Factor* **Referral Matrix®** .

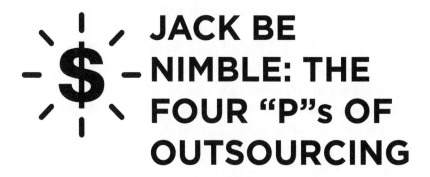

JACK BE NIMBLE: THE FOUR "P"s OF OUTSOURCING

IN THIS CHAPTER:

1. The Power of Outsourcing.
2. The Four Ps: Planning, Picking, Phasing in/out, and Partnering.

CHAPTER 7

I knew when I set out to write about small business success factors that I would have to include a chapter on outsourcing, but not for the reasons that you might think. I had no desire to add to the vast and growing canon of conventional wisdom, most of it offered by vendors — or outsourced vendors of vendors — trying to convince us to outsource business to

THEM. Time is limited. We get that. You'd have to be a wizard with some kind of time-turning device to personally check all the boxes on an entrepreneur's to-do list. And even if you could, why would you want to? This is a business, not a contest. Your objective should be to build the leanest, meanest, sustainable organization possible.

The Power of Outsourcing

But cash is also limited, especially during the pre-launch phase, before you've issued and collected on your first invoice. What entrepreneurs need is a methodology for organizing to-dos, and for determining which are must dos, which should be outsourced, and which could be done at a later date, or not at all. My 4P method does that.

You may have heard of the Four "P"s of marketing: Product, Price, Place, and Promotion. Given my bias for action, my four Ps are verbs, not nouns, and represent a four-step process for successful outsourcing: Planning, Picking, Phasing In/Out, and Partnering.

Step 1 – Planning

In the first step we outline the basic structures you will need in your business for it to be functional. This is unique to every business, but there are some basic areas that are common to all – invoicing, selling, taxes, accounting, etc. Begin this "Planning" phase by listing all the bases that need to be covered in your business, for example:

Prospecting	Accounting	Procurement
Selling	Bookkeeping	Industrial Design
Invoicing	Finances	Product development
A/R Management	Payroll	Code writing

Hiring	Publishing	IT
Training	Marketing communications	Warehouse management
Writing	Digital marketing	Delivery/ Logistics

Step 2 – Picking

The next step is the fun one. Here you will put the above items in an EXCEL spreadsheet and "Pick" the jobs you want to do by putting your name next to them. You should base your decisions on the following criteria:

- What do you do best?

- What do you like to do?

- What do you not like to do?

- What could you pay someone else to do cheaper?

- And, what else could you do, in a pinch, if you had to?

I included the last one in recognition of the fact that resources are limited and you may need to do certain things you may not want to do in the best interest of your company, until you have enough cash coming in to hand off to someone else. Assign ownership to these tasks using three distinct labels:

Three Labels Table

Me	These are things in your company that you'll do. Choose those things you do best, like, or can do in a pinch, if needed.
In-house	Activities to be handled by someone in your organization (Other than you).
Outsource	Things you don't like to do, and neither you, nor anyone in your organization is qualified to do, or, things than can be done by a third-party cheaper than it can be done in-house.

Picking Table

PLANNING	PICKING
Prospecting	Me
Selling	Me
Invoicing	In-house
A/R Management	In-house
Accounting	In-house
Bookkeeping	In-house
Payroll	In-house
Hiring	In-house
Training	In-house
IT	Outsource
Digital Marketing	In-house
Product Development	Me
Distribution	In-house
New Business Development	Me
Delivery / Logistics	Outsource
Writing / Blogging	Me

Step 3 - Phasing In/Out

Megatons of thrust are required for a rocket to break free of Earth's atmosphere. But once the rocket is in orbit, the fuel tanks and similar dead weight are cast off so that the rocket can maneuver more nimbly. Similarly, there are processes required at the launch of a business that are no longer necessary once the business is up and running. The third "P" pertains to "Phasing" tasks in and out, and could also reasonably be called "Pruning." For this step, add two more columns to your spreadsheet. Label the first column, "6 months," and the second, "1 year."

In these columns you will demarcate items you plan to bring in house, consolidate with other activities, or eliminate because they are no longer necessary. This is a discipline that even some of the world's biggest companies struggle to master, but it critical if you want your business to remain competitive.

Phasing In/Out Table

PLANNING	PICKING	PHASE IN/OUT 6 MONTHS	PHASE IN/OUT 1-YEAR	PARTNERING
Prospecting	Me	Me	In-house	In-house
Selling	Me	Me	In-house	In-house
Invoicing	In-house	In-house	In-house	In-house
A/R Management	In-house	Outsource	Outsource	Outsource
Accounting	In-house	In-house	Outsource	Partner
Bookkeeping	In-house	In-house	Outsource	Partner
Payroll	In-house	In-house	Outsource	Outsource
Hiring	In-house	In-house	In-house	In-house
Training	In-house	In-house	In-house	In-house
IT	Outsource	Outsource	Outsource	Outsource
Digital Marketing	In-house	In-house	Outsource	Outsource
Product Development	Me	In-house	In-house	Partner
Distribution	In-house	Outsource	Outsource	Partner
New Business Development	Me	Me	In-house	Partner
Delivery / Logistics	Outsource	Outsource	Outsource	Outsource
Writing / Blogging	Me	In-house	Outsource	Outsource

Step 4 – Partnering

The fourth and final P is Partnering. This is where you identify strategic third-party relationships that will add measurable value to your business by:

- Providing capabilities or services you would not otherwise be able to offer

- Filling a critical skills or talent gap

- Partnering with other small businesses to share the cost of non-core services and infrastructure

- Sharing office space, administrative personnel, Internet access, and IT infrastructure, with other businesses.

Partnering Table

PLANNING	PICKING	PHASE IN/OUT 6 MONTHS	PHASE IN/OUT 1-YEAR	PARTNERING
Prospecting	Me	Me	In-house	In-house
Selling	Me	Me	In-house	In-house
Invoicing	In-house	In-house	In-house	In-house
A/R Management	In-house	Outsource	Outsource	Outsource
Accounting	In-house	In-house	Outsource	Partner
Bookkeeping	In-house	In-house	Outsource	Partner
Payroll	In-house	In-house	Outsource	Outsource
Hiring	In-house	In-house	In-house	In-house
Training	In-house	In-house	In-house	In-house
IT	Outsource	Outsource	Outsource	Outsource
Digital Marketing	In-house	In-house	Outsource	Outsource
Product Development	Me	In-house	In-house	Partner
Distribution	In-house	Outsource	Outsource	Partner
New Business Development	Me	Me	In-house	Partner
Delivery / Logistics	Outsource	Outsource	Outsource	Outsource
Writing / Blogging	Me	In-house	Outsource	Outsource

This is, by no means, a comprehensive list. Your list will reflect the needs and profile of your business.

By using the four Ps, you can plan to do only those things you like, you're good at, and to which you add value within the realm of your company. You can identify processes you'd like to bring in-house, consolidate, or eliminate, and look for ways to share costs and resources with others through strategic and value-added partnerships. And you can outsource within the limitations of cash flow and budget.

Chapter 7 Success Factors

1. Use my 4 Ps of Outsourcing (Planning, Picking, Phasing In/Out, and Partnering) to determine what you should do yourself, and what should be outsourced.

2. Evaluate your processes after launch and prune those that are not needed to sustain a going concern.

3. Partner with other small businesses to share common overhead, such as administrative staff, communications systems, office space and IT infrastructure.

VIRTUALLY AWESOME . . . LITERALLY

IN THIS CHAPTER:

1. mCommerce – the Mobile Imperative.
2. Digital Strategy.
3. Website.
4. Social Media.
5. Electronic Mail.

CHAPTER 8

Conventional Wisdom Says:

Outbound marketing — paid advertising, cold calls, mass emails to purchased lists, direct mail, and telemarketing — is the best way to prospect for customers.

Unconventional Wisdom Says:

You need a digital strategy to attract and pre-qualify leads, and increase conversion rates at much lower acquisition cost than traditional outbound marketing.

My phone rang and the man on the other end identified himself as Armando. He was calling in the name of my banker, who had given him my contact. In somewhat broken English, he let me know he was heading down to Melbourne Beach for an appointment, and afterwards would be returning to town and wanted to stop by to see me.

A few hours later Armando showed up at my office. He worked in the disaster restoration business, which as one can imagine, in a state like Florida overrun with hurricanes and tropical storms, is a pretty good business. Switching into Spanish, which was his native language, he explained to me he had performed a number of restoration jobs recently, and was waiting to be paid. In his business, the insurance companies hire and pay for this type of work, but frequently their terms are upwards of 70 days. That's a long time to wait to get paid, especially, when you have other jobs in the pipeline, all of which require you to buy materials and pay for labor upfront, usually over several days while you perform the job. So very quickly, I figured out this gentleman needed money.

As part of the qualifying process, there are a number of forms which must be filled out, and if Armando came personally to my office, I wasn't going to let him leave without filling out the forms and providing me the documentation I needed for an initial evaluation. We sat down and got to work.

Once we completed the basic forms I turned to him and explained that I needed tax, banking, and company information. With that, he reached in his pocket and pulled out his smartphone. With his thick, hardened and weathered fingers, accustomed to working long hours underneath the hot Florida sun sawing, drilling, and nailing, he began searching for the information I requested. I thought to myself how different his hands were from mine, which were soft-skinned and pale, also accustomed to long hours, but in my case, underneath the white, indirect light of my office, scanning, faxing, and typing.

I began with banking information – his weathered index finger moved quickly to produce three months of statements. He sent them to my inbox, turned to me and said, *"Listo!"*, which in Spanish means "done" or "ready."

I then asked for Invoices — again, the index finger punched the glass surface of his phone in search of the documents and in no time, locating the half-dozen invoices proving he had executed the work. He turned to me again, and replied, *"Listo!"*

Next came my request for Purchase Orders. A few swipes, a couple of hard finger stabs, and then, *"Listo!"*

Thinking that this time, I would trick him, I asked for his income taxes. Out came that darn index finger again, surfing casually across the glass surface of his phone looking for his taxes. After only a few more moments, it successfully zeroed in on the location of the data. Hammering the phone almost with a vengeance with his right index finger, Armando turned to me again and said, *"Listo!"*

We finished up a few more things, and I turned to him and said that he had done his part, now it was my turn to do mine. (Meaning, I would prepare the necessary documentation and forward to underwriting for evaluation ASAP). We shook hands (again, those thick, weathered fingers), I thanked him for his visit, and returned to the comfort, soft indirect lighting, and background classical music of my office.

What impressed me more than anything about Armando's visit, was not his business, nor its potential for growth. No, what impressed me most was his darn phone! Armando was managing his entire company from his smartphone (and doing it with ease). This guy is not your techy, smartphone whiz-kid who spends his entire day on his phone looking up the latest and greatest in the Apps world. This is your everyday, nose to the grindstone, hardworking small business owner (but with thick, callused fingers) who very quickly and cleverly has figured out where the world is going: Mobile.

Look around! Everywhere people are sitting, walking, and not just talking, but using their smartphones for everything. They're researching, surfing, buying, interacting, gossiping, sitting in on podcasts and webinars, videos; you name it. And they're doing it all on their smartphones.

We are at the very beginning of a massive cultural, behavioral, and technological revolution, which has at its forefront, the smartphone and its mobile platforms and Apps. We've hardly just begun, and it's already taking over.

mCommerce — the Mobile Imperative

According to Forbes magazine, 9 out of 10 adults in the United States keeps a smartphone within reach at all times; 9 out of 10 mobile searches lead to action; and half of those actions are sales.

The world is in the middle of a massive mobile revolution, and interactions with customers need to be, not just informative, but also transactional. Customers want to hear about your company, research it on their hand-held devices, and then place an order and pay the bill. The National Retail Federation reports that 8 out of 10 consumers use their smartphone in-store for purchasing decisions.

When you think about the world of business, you have to understand it is a finite world, where resources are not unlimited. This is especially true for the small business owner. Your capital funding has its limits, and many of the most important and difficult decisions during early stages of your business have to do with the rationalization of funds. You want to fund everything, but your pockets are only so deep. So when it comes to your digital strategy, you are deciding between investing in one marketing area versus another, due to differences in strategy or desired outcome. But either way, you cannot invest in them all, and you have to choose. Given this situation, the unconventional wisdom offered in this book to you, the business owner, is to go deep, fast, and **first** into a mobile platform, even before your web platform. In the rationalization of funding of your overall digital strategy, favor and prioritize the resource spend toward your mobile platform first, before any other. Go mobile first, on order execution, demand generation, contact management, content generation, etc. Whatever it is, favor first your mobile platform, and once you've satisfied that, only then should you turn your efforts and remaining dollars to your Web-based strategies and resource spending.

So you as the business owner must build your platforms to cater to this population and their users. That means spending and rationalizing your marketing dollars in favor first of your mobile digital strategy, whatever that may be, whether that's:

- Selling homemade Thai sauces → mobile!

- Lead generation for organic wine-grape growers → mobile!

- Designing gluten-free customized cupcakes → mobile!

- Sourcing leather handbags from free-range cows → mobile!

Your mobile platform, right out of the blocks, must be built and tailor-made to your new business, whatever your product or service may be. That's the unconventional wisdom and what the smart businesses are doing today. *Listo!*

Digital Strategy

I don't hold myself out as a digital marketing guru, as my

background is in sales, finance, and operations. However, recognizing that your digital strategy is your company's online business model, there are, in my opinion, a few items which no small business or start-up (with the exception of a tech start-up) can do without. In addition to the unconventional wisdom on going mobile fast and first, your digital strategy must necessarily including the following pillars

1. A secure **Website** to serve as your online headquarters, communications hub, recruiting center, showroom, marketing kiosk, sales floor, customer service department, and vendor portal.

2. **Social media:** LinkedIn, Twitter and Facebook, are three "must-haves." You may add to these any social media your targeted customers use — to optimize search and increase your online reach and influence. Content on these platforms should be interesting and conversational, not salesy.

3. **An inbound** marketing strategy to engage prospects, generate sales leads, and convert them to customers.

These are the basics. There are some key elements to each, which I'll explore briefly.

Website

Here are five things every good small business website should have — with the caveat that, given the rapid pace of change, if you are reading this more than two years after the publication date, you should probably check to see what new capabilities have been added.

1. **Search Engine Optimization** — your site's online resume, designed to impress search engine "spiders" out looking for answers to life's persistent questions.

2. **Mobile-friendly design** — Typically, a one-page scrolling layout, with fonts and images aligned for easy navigation and readability on a smartphone or tablet. Search engines will only present mobile-friendly sites in response to mobile queries.

3. **Outbound marketing features** — to tag website visitors for targeted online advertising.

4. **Inbound conversion tools** — "calls to action" (CTA) urging visitors to email, register, call, or buy.

5. **A compelling offer** — free downloads, newsletters or webinars, in exchange for registration.

Search Engine Optimization (SEO)

Google and other search engine providers, have giant banks of computers — called "bots" or "spiders" — that "crawl" the internet every day looking for new websites, noting changes, and ranking existing sites using secret mathematical formulas designed to reward popular or particularly informative sites. Web pages are "indexed" and ranked according to key content tags, mobile-compatibility, loading speed, and readability.

A high search ranking can lead to more customer referrals, which has led some companies to look for ways to game the search process. Search engine providers are onto this trick and will de-list companies caught cheating. Avoid tricks intended to improve search engine rankings. A good rule of thumb is whether you'd feel comfortable explaining what you've done to a website that competes with you, or to a Google employee. Another useful test is to ask, "Does this help my users? Would I do this if search engines didn't exist?"

In order for your site to rank well in search results pages, it's important to make sure that Google can crawl and index your site correctly. Google's Webmaster Guidelines, available free online, outline some best practices that can help you avoid common pitfalls and improve your site's ranking.

Social Media

The internet is a community, with customs, hangouts, cliques, businesses, residents, and shady characters — just like any community. And, as you would interact with your physical community to connect and build your business, you need to interact with people online. As the name implies, social media is the vehicle for that.

There are any number of social media communities and clubs you can belong to. LinkedIn, Twitter, and Facebook are among the most popular, but I recommend asking your customers where they hang out online, and making sure that you, or your company become active in those communities. Keep in mind, however, that these are, in fact, communities, and conduct yourself as if you were conversing face to face. Think about what knowledge or service you have to offer the community and don't be too overtly self-interested. Be a giver, and your community members will be more likely to accept you and reward you with their business.

The main thing is to be authentic and to maintain a presence. Remember, nobody knows you're there until you speak. Nobody's going to listen unless you have something interesting to say. And they're going to be the judges of what's interesting to them.

It would take far more space than we have here to go over all your social media options. Suffice to say that it is possible, and advisable, to synchronize your efforts among platforms, using free "plug-in" functionality on your website to take posts from a single source — I recommend using your blog — and automatically share those posts with all of your social media accounts. It is also important to note that all of the major social networks have free built-in metrics to help you analyze your user demographics: when they are online, what part of the country they live in, and how they reacted to specific content. It is possible, using simple, and free, segmentation tools, to send different content to different groups, according to their respective interests. Segmentation is playing the digital game at the expert level, but it is highly effective because it helps you connect with prospective customers on a more personal level.

I have included some useful tips and tricks for some of the more popular social media below. Please keep in mind, as you read, that everything you do online, across platforms, must be well planned. It's one thing to come across as casual and spontaneous, but that should be a carefully considered decision.

LinkedIn

For business-to-business start-ups and professional services, LinkedIn is the best resource for free or low-cost customer relationship management, prospecting, thought leadership, and client/vendor research. One nice feature is the ability to see who have visited your page, allowing you to follow up with them.

LinkedIn, like most social media networks, also offers easy-to-read dashboard reporting on ad campaigns, and A-B testing, allowing you to test viewer reactions so various ads and determine which generate the best response. This is great for new businesses which may be fine-tuning their product/service offering.

Tips and Tricks: (from LinkedIn)

1. Human vs object – Images of people generate significantly better results.

2. Light or dark background – Given similar images, darker

background images result in 33% more clicks.

3. Terms – Given the choice to download an "ebook" or a "guide" (with the exact same content), people choose "guide" with a 95% click-through rate.

4. Statistics – Captions with stats show better click-through rates and conversions.

5. Links – shorter links (less than 150 characters) show higher click through rates.

6. Gaze – Draw your reader's eye to the "action button" by having the person in the ad look at it. The direction of the model's gaze has a big impact on clicks, with 76% effectivity.

7. Calls to action – Test several terms for the call to action, to see whether, "click here," "learn more," or "go to" work better for your target audience.

8. Kitchen sink – While it is best to test your ads by only changing one element at a time, if the budget is tight, you can test as many different elements as possible with one test.

9. Remember that the visual "image" is the new "headline."

10. Test, track, and understand the results of your testing to optimize results.

When planning a LinkedIn ad campaign, remember to determine your objective, test the ad elements, align the content with targeting strategy, and don't be afraid to experiment.

Twitter

If you thought Twitter was just for young folks with short attention spans, consider the revolution in political strategies that occurred when President Donald Trump decided to bypass traditional media in favor of going straight to the American people with his announcements and opinions. The jury is still out on whether it is a strategy for better or worse, but you certainly have to admit that there are very few citizens of voting age in America, from 18 to 80, who don't now know what a "tweet" is.

It's also possible for Twitter users to bring a great deal of positive or negative attention to your company with a well-phrased, well-timed message of 140 characters or less. Make sure that incoming and outgoing tweets are monitored carefully and consistently, so that problems can be addressed in a timely, professional manner, and relationships can be nurtured with existing and potential clients. A complaint that is ignored on Twitter can bring a company to its knees, but a complaint that is handled quickly and well can convert not only the original complainer, but the legions who read the complaint and your response, into loyal customers.

A very important feature that originated with Twitter and has spread to other networks, is the use of a "#" symbol, or "hashtag" preceding a word, to serve as a common search reference for trending topics, boosting your reach beyond those who have subscribed to your page ("followers" in Twitter-speak). This has become especially popular for topical content, such as keynote speakers or vendors reaching out to attendees at a particular conference, and as a way for those who didn't attend a conference to keep up on industry highlights.

Facebook

No longer simply a place to post pictures of your food, or a riveting video loop of your cat chasing its tail, Facebook was similarly used by former President Barack Obama to galvanize a nation behind his message of hope and change with the ubiquitous catchphrase, "Yes We Can." More personal than LinkedIn (with its businesslike invitation to "connect"), Facebook is primarily a platform for "friends" to "like" one another's pages and posts. But businesses are learning to use it as a way to promote their softer, philanthropic and altruistic side. It is also a great place to promote scholarships, contests, webinars and other events. Failing to have a presence on Facebook means that the millions of potential customers who use Facebook as their preferred — or only — social media platform will not find you there, and will therefore possibly not consider your business relevant.

When establishing your Facebook strategy, Doyle Buehler, author of *The Digital Delusion: How to Overcome the Misguidance & Misinformation Online,* advises you to figure out what your goal is before you get started. Do you want likes, shares, or commentary? If you want likes, issue a call to action that begins, "LIKE THIS IF...." If you want comments, ask a question. And if you want shares, discuss topics regarding your brand or market niche, and always use short links back to a website that has more information.

Doyle also advises choosing topics people care about, writing a compelling headline, making posts skim-able, with plenty of graphics and pictures, and ensuring they can be easily shared. Avoid being selfish – he suggests a ratio of 10% your content and 90% sharing of others' content, with attribution to the original author/poster and a link back to their material or website. Doyle wants you to know that videos are shared twelve times more than links and text posts, and that YouTube is the second largest search engine. He says 70% of business-to-business (B2B) online ads include video. Want one final piece of unconventional wisdom from Doyle? "Social media ROI is a marathon, not a sprint."

Even if you outsource your social media presence, as I suggested in the chapter on Outsourcing, because you have more important things to do than spending your day online, monitor your social media platforms and presence frequently to be sure your delegates are managing things the way you would like. It's your company's reputation on the line, after all, and public opinion can bring a company down, or lift it to new heights, with a tweet or a post.

Electronic Mail

Electronic mail (email) has replaced direct mail (junk mail) as the marketing medium of choice for businesses looking to connect with customers beyond their physical reach. But while it may be tempting to run out and buy, or rent, an email list, I would strongly advise against it.

The best part of direct mail was that it allowed businesses to target specific zip codes, and even sub-zips, based on demographics such as age and income. The power of email marketing is that it takes that targeting ability all the way down to the individual email account within a household, and with proper targeting — using opt-in emails provided by individuals that have visited your website — it has been shown to yield a 95 times better return on investment than direct mail, according to a 2016 survey by HubSpot, a leading provider and authority on inbound marketing strategy.

Email acquisition should be one of the primary objectives of your other online activities, because it is through email, and the related demographic information volunteered by inbound prospects as part of your engagement strategy, that you turn prospects to leads, and begin the process of converting as many as possible to customers. A final word of advice, before we move into some of the particulars: Tend your email garden with care. Most people already get more email than they can manage. They have trusted you with this direct line into their phone or desktop. You need to respect their time and prove yourself to be email worthy. Use this opportunity to build a relationship. Don't sell — at least not in the body of your email. Give them news they can use, with a relevant offer from you as a secondary, or even tertiary focus. Remember what I said about win/win. Don't make it about you.

I know that's counterintuitive — you might even call it "unconventional." But that's how the dance is done, according to my good friend, tennis ace and email wizard Cathy Cain-Black, president of CC Marketing and Communication, who handles my Liquid Capital email campaigns.

Email Marketing Programs

In the eyes of Cain-Black, a well-crafted email marketing campaign must contain the following elements:

1. **List** — Develop a mailing list that includes the first and last names of the individual, the name of the business, and the individual's email address. Business owners who, due to time or money constraints, need to wait before launching an email program should nevertheless start building this list on day one. It's okay to start this list in Excel. Once you're ready to start your campaign, your list can be uploaded to an email platform, such as Constant Contact, MailChimp, or Infusion Soft. Keeping multiple lists, say in Outlook and QuickBooks, for instance, is

not recommended as that could result in duplicate and outdated records. Keep the list clean! Incorrect email addresses can bounce back and get your emails labeled as spam with some delivery systems, undermining your efforts, time, and precious dollars. Ideally everyone on the list should have "opted in," meaning that they have agreed to receive mailings from you. This is an important step, and one that will significantly improve readership and engagement with your emails.

2. **Welcome email** — To kick off the business relationship with the people on your contact list, you need a welcome email that is generic enough that it doesn't become dated in any way, no matter when it goes out. This should typically go out the first time someone registers for a newsletter or downloads free content from your site. The welcome message should be the first in a scripted series of automated responses, timed over several weeks, reaching out to prospects from a variety of angles, trying to get them to engage and act. Remember to include a useful download or special offer, so that people are happy to see your email in their inbox, and will actually open and read it.

3. **Schedule** — Set up a production schedule for emails that includes writing the text, developing appropriate images and graphics, editing all of the above, and sending them out on a regular basis. It's important to vary the mix, too – for example, between newsletters, success stories, and blogs.

4. **Automate** — By automating repetitive tasks like email campaigns, you can control the intervals when they are sent, and load subsequent emails at the beginning of the month or week, without having to remember to do it during the course of a busy workday. Cathy recommends

a frequency of at least once a month, and more often if your competitors do so, or if you have an announcement to make. She also says you should get on your competitors' mailing lists so that you'll know what they are saying, and how often. Each email should contain something of value, like helpful tips or attractive offers.

You should not always push your products or services in your emails; they should often address concerns, solve problems, or simply entertain. This will keep you top of mind, engage you in conversations with current or prospective clients, and generate referrals. Eventually, you should become known as a subject-matter-expert, and could be asked for interviews and to speak at topical events.

Whether you go solo or hire someone like Cathy to do it for you, make sure the person in charge of your program actually understands how the technology works and what you can and cannot do. (Emails may render differently in Outlook than in Gmail or Yahoo, for example, and you want to be sure that all of your campaigns are mobile friendly.) An experienced email marketing company will know how to modify a template or troubleshoot to ensure your emails look good to all email clients and on different devices.

Understand that "doing it yourself" (DIY) may not be the best approach to email marketing programs, and you may not want to go with the smallest, cheapest local service provider. Find out, at the very least, whether your provider has a good relationship with the companies that will send the emails out. The CAN - SPAM Act, a law that sets compliance rules for commercial email, has tough penalties for violations, and one or two spam complaints out of a thousand emails sent can get a company put on the spam list and ruin its deliverability rate. An email service provider may also close the email account of any company or individual that doesn't follow the rules. So investigate first, and choose your provider based not just on cost, but also on competence.

If your campaign is sent out via email to 1,000 people, and 100 open the email, that's a 10 percent open rate — keep in mind that your actual readership will be higher than that because many email users read their email in the preview pane. Of those that opened the message, if 50 click through to apply for an interview with your company, that's a five percent click-through rate. Out of those 50, maybe 10 will qualify for a sales appointment. If you close 6 out of those 10 qualified customers, you've got a 60 percent close ratio.

So what does all that mean? It means that much of what conventional wisdom would consider marketing has already moved online. Email has replaced direct marketing as companies increasingly use social media, SEO, and website "calls to action." Mass marketing and "cold calling" of random names or numbers, has given way to more targeted digital campaigns sent to self-selecting "warm" inbound prospects, already familiar with the company through online interactions.

So whether you hire a pro who will go the extra mile to make you, your company, and your campaigns look their best, or do it yourself, make sure you follow the basic steps outlined in this chapter. By merely doing so, you will be well on your way to reaping the rewards from following unconventional wisdom in your digital strategy.

Chapter 8 Success Factors

1. A digital strategy, including a mobile-friendly platform and inbound marketing, is absolutely essential if your business is going to survive and thrive.

2. A website should serve as your online headquarters, communications hub, recruiting center, showroom, marketing kiosk, sales floor, customer service department, and vendor portal.

3. Mass marketing, and cold-calling, have been replaced with targeted and hyper-personal online engagement strategies designed to convert "warm leads" into customers.

CASH IS KING. DON'T BE A PAWN.

IN THIS CHAPTER:

1. What is factoring?
2. How factoring works.
3. What's in a name?
4. Why choose factoring?
5. So, who needs factoring?

Conventional Wisdom Says:

Use bank financing to meet all your businesses liquidity needs.

Unconventional Wisdom Says:

Factoring is not an after-thought. Use it from Day 1 of your new business to provide you the working capital and liquidity you need to grow your business to success.

You created something of value, developed a business model, followed your timeline, and went for it. Few things are as exhilarating as that first puff of wind in your sails as you embark on your entrepreneurial journey.

So there you are. Out in the deep water. You send out your first invoices, and . . . wait.

You've got a payroll to meet. The landlord stops by, "just to see how you're doing," wink, wink. Another order comes in, but you won't have the cash to buy raw materials until you get paid for what you've already shipped. Depending on the industry, that could be 30, 60, or even 90 days. And that's assuming everyone pays on time — or pays at all. You did remember to check the credit of those customers you so eagerly signed, right?

How deep are your pockets? Will you have to max out your credit cards? Your banker is unlikely to be able to help you further given your new business or start-up status. You start to wonder how much the flat screen television in the employee break room might fetch on eBay?

There's a simple solution that may not have occurred to you. You may not even be aware of it. It's called factoring. You could sell your invoices. That's right. There are companies out there, such as my company, Liquid Capital, that will buy your invoices, advance you between 75-80% of the invoice value, providing you the cash for working capital almost immediately after you've sold and delivered your product or services. When the end customer finally pays the invoice, you receive the balance minus the fees for factoring. It's fast, not new debt or a term loan, and can grow in size along with the growth of your business. Factoring. It may be the best piece of unconventional wisdom I have to offer you.

What is Factoring?

If you've never heard of factoring, don't feel bad. Most people haven't — although the industry has been around since 2,000 B.C. I'm often surprised when people HAVE heard of it.

Recently I was making small talk with a woman on a rental car shuttle bus, who told me she was a vice president at a large national bank. She asked what I did for a living and I told her, "I'm a factor." With a blank look on her face, she asked, "What's a factor?" Hmmm, I thought, and to think, bankers are some of my best referral partners.

When a financial services professional doesn't know what a factor is, you can see why I felt compelled to close this book with an explanation, and a challenge for you to explore what I believe to be the best financial option for small business growth.

How Factoring Works

As I mentioned, factoring has been around for thousands of years. Modern factoring began in England in the 1300s as a cash flow solution for clothing merchants, who needed money to buy cloth and thread, but had all their cash tied up in inventory. It came to the New World in the 1600s, when American colonists needed advance payments on raw materials like corn, wool, timber, tobacco, and cotton shipped across the Atlantic Ocean to England.

Today factoring is a 3-trillion-dollar industry worldwide and is one of the most popular business financing options in Europe because it allows companies to get their own cash fast, without going into debt. It has been catching on here in the United States, especially since the credit crunch of 2008. But it is still not widely understood.

Here's how it works. Let's say you're in your first year of business, after your start-up as a supplier of linens to hotels and restaurants. You've diligently followed the unconventional wisdom laid out in the pages of this book related to your value proposition, business models, timelines, referral marketing, and digital strategies, to name just a few. You're up and running, sales are in place and you're invoicing $10,000 a month. You're providing services to some larger hotels and overall, your receivables average 45 days outstanding. Your small company is growing, taking on new clients, new employees, and needs cash, so you turn to factoring. You call on your friend at Liquid Capital

FACTORING: HOW DOES IT WORK?

Clients Monthly Sales		$10,000
Accounts Receivable Outstanding (days) **45D**		$15,000
Advance Amount	**80.0%**	**$12,000**

Monthly Factoring Costs Based on Outstanding A/R

Rate for 30 Days		**2.0%**
First 30 Days		$200
Additional Days		$100
Total Factoring Cost	**$300**	
Amount Paid by Customers at 45 Days	$15,000	
Balance Forwarded by Liquid Capital (net of funds cost)	$2,700	**($3000 - $300)**
Total Funds Received From Factoring	**$14,700**	**($12000 + $2700)**

(me) who explains that he can advance 80% on your $10,000 worth of monthly invoices, which average 45 days outstanding, thus purchasing them from you. Once your customers pay him, he forwards you the balance (remaining 20%), minus a fee of 2% per each 30 days. The calculation looks like this:

The advance amount on $10,000 in monthly invoices, 45 days outstanding, is $12,000 (1½ months x $10,000 x 80% = $12,000). Your friendly Liquid Capital principal charges you 2% on the first 30 days (2% x $10,000) + 2% for 15 additional days, which is 2% x (½ x $10,000) = $200 + $100 = $300.00. At 45 days, when the customer pays Liquid Capital, you receive the balance owed you ($15,000 - $12,000 = $3,000) minus the cost of the funds ($300) or $2,700. You will have received $14,700 on your $15,000 worth of invoices, at a cost of only $300.

What's in a Name?

So why isn't factoring more popular? One easy explanation relates to advertising. As we all know, advertising is fundamental to brand awareness — banks, insurance companies, financial service firms all use it. But I challenge you to recall the last time you saw an advertisement on factoring.

In an attempt to enhance further their awareness, many lawyers in my hometown have made the "bus door" the preferred method of advertising. I can just imagine the initial conversation between a prospective slip-and-fall client and their new lawyer: "So how did you hear about me?" And the prospective client answers, "I saw you on the bus! Well not literally 'on the bus', but on the bus. You get what I mean, right?" I'm not making a case to use this same form of advertising for factoring, but clearly my industry has a need to up the ante, get its name out there, and more effectively increase awareness of the tremendous service and benefits it provides to small businesses, helping them to grow and succeed.

Why Choose Factoring?

To help you better understand the overall benefits this type of financing can provide your business, I'm going to serve up what I call the **Seven Famous Reasons** why a company would want to use factoring to meet its working capital needs.

1. **Growth** — This is the best reason to need money. Your company is growing; congratulations! Do you want to keep growing? If the answer is yes (and I sincerely hope it is, or you've wasted your money buying this book), then you need to find a source of immediate cash to finance your growth.

2. **Liquidity** — Cash is the lubricant that keeps the wheels of commerce turning. You might need immediate cash for any number of valid reasons, including:

- Buying raw materials
- Employee payroll
- Paying taxes
- Hiring a project team
- Purchasing electronic, print, or digital media
- Paying a large bill
- Funding a shortfall
- Buying new equipment
- Paying for a new computer system (ERP, WMS, etc.) or operating licenses.

The list goes on. The needs for cash in a small business are endless, and are unique to each business. Factoring makes it easy to pay for those needs with cash you've already earned, without having to go into debt.

3. **New company** — In my practice at Liquid Capital in Central Florida, I frequently see businesses drawn to the area by the theme parks, hotel industry, booming timeshare offerings, and a growing technology sector driven by simulation and animation. When your company is new, and hasn't yet established a credit history, because it simply hasn't been operating long enough, you will have capital challenges. Factoring is a perfect way to bridge that cash gap until you can establish a track record.

4. **Banks say no** — Since the financial crash of 2008 and the global recession it caused, banks are under increasing

pressure to comply with tightened regulations. The Dodd-Frank Act, intended to prevent another crash, ushered in a new regimen of risk analysis, stress-testing, and strict rules on the types of credit risks that banks can take with federally insured deposits. A bank that a decade ago might have provided an entrepreneur with a $50,000 unsecured revolving credit line, at 8 percent interest, with no upfront fee, today might charge 4 percent up front for a $25,000 cash advance, at 15 percent interest, and require a $100,000 certificate of deposit as collateral. When a bank requires a $100,000 down payment to borrow $25,000, at credit card interest rates, you can see why trading $10,000 in monthly invoices payable in 45 days, for cash now, as shown by our example, makes sense.

5. **Too much debt** — In the 1987 film, Wall Street, when Michael Douglas's character Gordon Gekko bragged, "Greed is good," he could easily have added, "and debt is good, too," because so many companies inadvertently get themselves into trouble by taking on too much debt.

6. **Balance sheet** — Here you simply may not present sufficient assets, including cash, accounts receivable, inventory, or machinery & equipment, to collateralize debt. As a result, you'll get politely shut down by your bank.

7. **Blemish** — A blemish on your credit history could be a bankruptcy (either of the company or one of its primary shareholders), or perhaps a legal dispute (with a bank, lending institution, or supplier) arising from an unpaid debt. Either way, it spells "R-I-S-K," and limits your borrowing potential.

Those are all pretty good reasons, and if I sit down with someone who has never heard of factoring, I can make the case in no time at all. The people I have trouble with are the ones who haven't personally ever looked into factoring, but refuse to consider it, because of some myth or misconception, the most common being:

- **My business is not distressed, so I don't need alternative financing.** — Factoring is not about providing funding to distressed companies. It's about helping companies free up cash they've already earned to grow, or to get them through a cash drought. A lot of very healthy companies will factor invoices in January, a transition month where customers can be slow to pay.

- **My customers will think I'm in trouble if I outsource my accounts receivables management. (This is factoring's version of "What will the neighbors think?")** — Actually, for many companies, there is an accounts payable department (or at least an AP clerk) that handles payments, so most company leaders don't involve themselves directly in how their bills are paid. And you might be surprised to learn that your customer himself has been using factoring for years.

- **I don't need it now — maybe later.** — If you are growing, or want to grow, NOW is the ideal time to factor. Or are you telling me you want to postpone your company's growth? Maybe you're waiting for a better astrological month? (Is Pisces better for business growth than Sagittarius?) The time is now! Growth happens – and then it doesn't. So if you are waiting for a better moment in time to use alternative financing, you may just miss the bus, and not have cash when you need it.

- **It's too expensive. The rates, the hidden fees, and the penalties will eat into my margins, so I'll stick with the financing I have.** — This is a common mistake, and one

I hope the examples below will put to rest. All financial services cost money, but some are more transparent than others. Some costs may not stand out on your profit and loss (P&L) statement as clearly as others do, but they are there. They may be in the form of payroll costs for a clerk of a department, or in employee benefits, or in increased bad debt expense, but all financial services cost money. It's just a matter of making sure that the benefits outweigh the costs.

Here are some comparative costs for different forms of financing:

Factoring vs. Bank Loan

Example: $100K loan from a bank, will cost 3.75% + Prime (3.75%), or 7.5%. Over 10 years, that will cost you $211,206.40, so you will effectively pay $111K for a loan that originally cost you $100,000. Factoring $100K at 2% for 30 days will cost you $2,000 — period.

Factoring vs. Credit Card Example:

A credit card costs 17.5% annually Do you really think credit cards are a viable option?

Factoring vs. PayPal

PayPal provides a sliding cost scale, which increases depending on the type of method you use to take payment for services. Here is the most recent cost chart (March 2017):

- Swiped invoices: 2.4%
- Invoices paid online: 2.9%
- Keyed invoices: 3.4%

What's really strange here is how they justify charging you more if you have to key in the invoice amounts (I guess that's how they punish you for not using their technology). These are not cheap fees. When I compare these charges to factoring — which includes credit analysis, underwriting, aging of receivables, and collection services for much less — I have a hard time buying the "your services are expensive" claims by some prospective clients. When I couple the above figures to the fact that PayPal is now at $10.4 billion in annual sales (2016), with a market capitalization of $52 billion, my answer is: you get what you pay for, and PayPal is laughing all the way to the bank as it charges very large fees for very little servicing. That's a lot of people using their services, so I guess they're not complaining too much.

Factoring vs. a Small Business Administration (SBA) Loan

Here are some of the typical covenants you will find collateralizing the Federal Government's SBA endorsed loans from your bank:

- 1.1.1 The Collateral shall consist of all now owned and hereafter acquired and wherever located personal property of Debtor

- 1.1.2 Accounts, including all contract rights and receivables;

- 1.1.3 Inventory, Including all returned inventory

- 1.1.4 Equipment, including all Accessories thereto, and all manufacturer's warranties, parts and tools therefore specifically described . . .

Basically, the Federal Government, through the Small Business Association, so tightly collateralizes its loans it literally takes away your right to your very own assets. These covenants prohibit factoring, cash advances, or asset based loans. Matt Damon, on his best day as Jason Bourne, couldn't get you out of the hold an SBA endorsed loan puts on your small business. Are you sure you want that?

In situations where I need to answer these concerns, I have my clients fill out the paperwork and at least get a financing facility approval. This way, you can choose to use it, or not. And the proverbial, "it will be there when you need it," holds true. But that still begs the question: Why wait? It's your own money that we factors are advancing to you. You're just getting it quicker.

One last thing before I get down off my soapbox. Einstein is often quoted as having said that the definition of insanity is doing the same thing, the same way, over and over again, and expecting different results. I find that some people are so stuck in their conventional thinking that they just can't get out of their own way. Here are four bad mistakes that business owners end up making because they can't manage to get their heads around factoring:

1. They take on more debt when they need money, instead of getting their own money faster by factoring.

2. They ignore collections efforts (because they consider their customers to be trustworthy friends), and then panic and despair when they don't get paid.

3. They fear what their customers will think if they factor their invoices, but then they have to delay completion of projects because they don't have enough money to hire the necessary personnel, because they didn't get paid.

4. They feel frustrated because they never reach the growth potential that alternative financing provides. The result is unfulfilled dreams for them, their business, and their employees, which leads to turnover, lackluster sales, and a feeling of disappointment in the business they once so enthusiastically endorsed.

Moving right along . . .

So, Who Needs Factoring?

Who needs it? You do.

One of the biggest challenges of alternative financing, and in particular, factoring, is convincing a start-up or small business that they really need it. In my practice at Liquid Capital, I run across many different types of businesses, and while doing this, one of the first topics of conversation almost always centers on financing needs. Based on my experience, today, I can very quickly assess a company and pretty much categorize most any company's business situation and need for alternative financing, into one of four basic categories. This **'Category Method®'** is what I use to assess prospective clients, and its description and examples follow:

4 Basic Customer Categories for Factoring:

1. Need cash — plain and simple.
2. Business model mandate.
3. Thanks, but I've got my own cash. (Blissfully unaware.)
4. Big customers, slow payers.

Category 1: Need cash — plain and simple

You remember Armando from our discussion on a Mobile Digital strategy, don't you? Well, his was a classic Category 1 situation with not much to explain — he needed cash, and needed it immediately. His situation springs from your garden variety type of small business problem where you offer your Customers say 30 or 45 day payment terms, while your business, on the other hand, pays its bills `due on receipt,' or usually within 15-20 days of receipt. If we do the math, sooner or later, the inevitable happens, and by you paying out faster than your receipts for sales, you find your business is strapped for cash.

The first analysis I do for any prospective client is determine their **Days Sales Outstanding, or DSO** (also known as 'days receivables'). DSO is the average number of days that a company's accounts receivables remain outstanding before they get paid. The calculation looks like this:

DAYS SALES OUTSTANDING (D.S.O.)

Definition: ⋯⋯⋯⋯⋯⋯⋯⋯⋯⋯⋯⋯⋯⋯⋯⋯⋯⋯⋯

$$DSO = \frac{\text{Accounts Receivables}}{\text{Sales}} \times 365 \text{ DAYS}$$

Example: ⋯⋯⋯⋯⋯⋯⋯⋯⋯⋯⋯⋯⋯⋯⋯⋯⋯⋯⋯

$$DSO = \frac{\$101{,}917.81}{\$1{,}200{,}000.00} \times 365$$

DSO = 31 Days

DSO is the key figure which tells us how many days a company takes to collect revenue after making a sale. It also is a measure of how effective a company's credit and collection efforts are, since your company is effectively extending credit to your trusted customers, and subsequently, collecting on those sales at some time (determined by you in your sales terms) in the future.

Upon performing a quick DSO calculation, I determine if a prospective client has passed the threshold for needing cash, or what I call "Category 1 status". In my practice, a company which has a DSO > 31 days, is labeled as "Category 1" and is a prime candidate for factoring services, since sooner or later, it will need cash for their continuing operations.

What's so special about a DSO >31 days? A company's normal operation occurs over a 30-day cycle. You sell, pay employees, make payroll, pay taxes, pay bills, and in general run your business within this 30 day window. If your sales receipts occur within this 30 day window, then assuming you have sufficient margins (defined as at least 20% gross margins) on your sales, you will more than likely, barring certain extraordinary items, have sufficient cash revenue to cover your monthly payables demands, and everything is peachy. If, however, your sales receipts fall outside of this period, into the next month (example, >30 days), then your company's cash receipts do not occur in the same time period as your payables, you will, all things being equal, find you are in a net negative cash flow position.

For large publicly traded and privately held companies with a mixed source of debt and equity to finance their operations, this is no problem. But for the small business owner, whose resources are finite and limited, depending on the size of the difference between payables and receivables, and the period over which this occurs, this can stretch and stress your financial reserves, or even in certain situations, be disastrous to you and your company.

So if, upon first blush, taking the DSO pulse, I see that your Days Receivables are over 31 days, I will label your business as a Category 1 client, with an imminent cash need, of which factoring represents a viable solution to solve your cash needs.

Category 2: Business model mandate

Business models are a bit like children – some are just plain more complicated than others. So if you have a complicated business model, no need to fret, because there are solutions to your cash flow problems. With respect to your children, that's another issue, but also as a parent, rest assured, you are not alone regarding challenges related to children, because as we say in Portuguese, "the problems we have with our kids are all the same, they just change address."

Category 2 customers actually represent a pretty straightforward solution, because the need, or 'pain point,' is so real and well defined. It just needs a bit of explaining. The 1994 film "Philadelphia," gave Tom Hanks an Academy Award for Best Actor, but the actor who stole the show was Denzel Washington, as Hanks' lawyer, who would say, "explain this to me like I'm a 2-year-old, because there's an element in this thing that I cannot get through my thick head." In Category 2 situations, due to the complexities of the model your business is predicated upon, the best solution for resolving the impasse, is a simple one: factoring.

Category 2 customers with their complicated business models, delve into another metric used to assess the needs of prospective clients, and that is the *Cash Conversion Cycle* (CCC). The cash conversion cycle is a number that measures the number of days a company's cash is tied up in inventories and accounts receivable. If your money is tied up in inventory and accounts receivables, it can't be used for making payroll, buying raw materials, hiring personnel, or any other use. It's stuck there for those days, unless you have another option to reduce that period – and that's where factoring comes in.

Let's take a look at an example of a Category 2 business model to show you what I mean.

Baby Jane Furnishings buys children's furniture from a terrific manufacture in Vietnam called 'Yo Man Products'. They have been working together for several years and have established a trusted business relationship. Yo Man requires a 30% down payment on a $60,000 order from Baby Jane, and delivers the finished product 30 days later to Cai Mep port in Vietnam. From there, it's collected by Baby Jane and off it goes for the 20-day trip across the Pacific to Oakland, California, where, once landed, it is funneled into Baby Janes logistics system for sale and delivery, with an attractive 40% Gross Margin (GM) to a large, regional U.S. retailer for the amount of $100,000.00.

The timeline for the operation described above looks like the following:

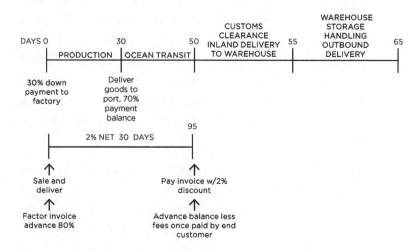

- Production lead time: **30 days**

- Ocean transit: **20 days**

- Customs clearance, Inland transport to Warehouse delivery: **5 days**

- Days in warehouse before sale: **10 days** (hypothetical, and depends on the minimum inventory levels used in your industry, but for our example, we'll keep it simple and use only 10 days.)

- Payment term on Sale, Invoice, Delivery: **30 days**

- Total time of cash cycle: **95 days**

From the moment Baby Jane plops down her 30% down payment, and completes payment of the balance (70%) 30 days later at delivery to port in Cai Mep, the total time her cash will be outstanding is a whopping 95 days. Now Baby Jane may have deep pockets, but most small companies don't; or if they can do it on the initial purchase order, they cannot repeat it for the 2nd and successive purchase orders.

This is where companies like mine, Liquid Capital (LC), come in to factor the receivables generated from the sale. At sale, LC buys the invoice from Baby Jane, and then advances 80% of the value of the receivable, or $80,000 to Baby Jane. Since Baby Jane sells at 40% GM, it now has $60,000 to place its next order with Yo Man, and still have $20,000 to make payroll, pay for warehousing, transport, or other service costs which are part of the operation. In 30 days, when the retail company pays LC the $100,000 invoice, LC then advances the balance to Baby Jane, minus its fee of 2% for 30 days. The balance paid to Baby Jane, or $18,000, is net of our fee (2% of $100,000 or $2,000.00) and goes back into her operation to complement the $80,000 already advanced, all of which is used to continue the cycle of purchase orders, import, customs clearance, warehousing, etc.

After discussing the mechanism of how factoring works to solve a business owner's cash flow dilemma, which stems from the type of business model employed, he or she quickly sees and understands that not only do they need factoring, but it is essential to the future success and growth of their small business. The long lead times between production and delivery, coupled to upfront down payments to factory to secure production, create costs and risks. This situation, when coupled at the end to sales to large customers, who because they're big, dictate payment terms favorable to them (and not you – remember we discussed this earlier in Chapter 5), creates a cash flow powder keg solved most easily by a factoring solution like that shown previously.

When explained clearly and succinctly, maybe so well it's even "clear to a 2-year old", like in Denzel's case, a Category 2 customer instantly realizes the value factoring brings to the health of his operation. Now that's unconventional wisdom even a 2-year old can understand.

Category 3: Thanks, but I've got my own cash

My friend and colleague, Topher Morrison, at Key Person of Influence, in Tampa, Florida refers to Category 3 Customers as `blissfully unaware.' He calls them that because they are unaware of the need they have for a service, and as a result, make for one of the toughest type of customer to sell to.

Category 3 Customers are blinded by their own success (i.e., money in the bank), puff up their chest, and basically say, "Your financing is for those poor souls who haven't been as successful in life as me, so thank you, but no thanks, I've got my own cash and don't need your service."

Now I don't take this personally. And neither should you, if I turn around and tell you that you do need me. And need me bad. Why? For any of three reasons. You may:

1. Lack the platform to perform the operation.

2. Lack the method to mitigate risk of the sales operation.

3. Underestimate the real cost of money.

Let me explain.

Reason #1 — Lack the platform to perform the operation

One of the most important services companies like mine perform is providing the platform or background for your sales activities, facilitating receipt of sales revenue efficiently, quickly, and safely. We do this by performing due diligence on your customers; analyzing their creditworthiness, backgrounds, payment histories, and in the end, establishing credit limits for each. We manage the Accounts Receivables into groups of when they are going to be paid, or "age" them and then actually do the collections associated with the receivables. This is the platform a company specializing in this service offers, that an individual business owner does not.

Reason #2 — Lack a method to mitigate risk of the sales operation

Companies in alternative financing, like Liquid Capital, have longstanding relationships with very special insurers, which offer credit insurance to cover sales transactions. With this, the credit risk of a customer is reduced substantially, and provides protection in two instances: 1) Failure or bankruptcy of the customer to which the sale was made, and 2) Protracted payment beyond the terms specified in the sales agreement. In these two cases, credit insurance can be employed to recover potentially lost sales dollars while at the same time, reduce the risk of future ones.

Reason #3 — Underestimate the real cost of money

It is the rare small business owner who realistically costs out his money. His view is always skewed to a comparison of mortgage rates or some other long-term loan, and as a result, he underestimates the direct costs as well as the opportunity costs of his money.

I illustrate a more realistic view of the cost of money with the following rationale:

- 25-year Average annual return Dow Jones Industrial Average: **10.6%** (7.9% stocks plus 2.7% Dividend return)

- Stock trade costs buy/sell: **2.5%**

I work with both Merrill Lynch and Morgan Stanley and they charge similar rates, around 1.25% a trade. This analysis ignores the low cost day-trading services like eTrade, TD Ameritrade, which I don't do.

- Bad debt cost (estimate): **1.0%**

Since the business owner is opting to finance with his own funds, the risk is all his own. In the likelihood of a default, the cost will be the business owner's, and let's estimate this cost to be 1% annually.

TOTAL COST: **14.1% annually or 1.18% per month**

Considering that Factoring costs vary between 1.5% - 2.5% per month, but offers the added services of due diligence, credit analysis, aging analysis, underwriting, collections, and the option of credit insurance against the receivables, my advice would be to keep your money invested in the Dow and employ the services of a trusted and experienced factoring company. If you need a recommendation, I know a good one.

Category 4: Big customers, slow payers

If big customers represent 20% or more of your total sales turnover, you need factoring. I use 20% as the line in the sand for determining whether a prospective client is a Category 4 customer or not. Big companies — this list includes hotels, retailers, insurance companies, utilities, and various government entities (federal, state, municipal) — are notoriously slow payers. In my practice, I define a "Slow Payer" as any customer who pays longer than 40 days.

When you sell to big customers, you need cash to fill their big orders — cash to buy inventory, raw materials, hire employees, service the customer, amongst other things. The sales to these customers are big, but the costs to attend them are also big. Factoring provides you the liquidity to adequately service and sell to your larger accounts, and avoiding that your big customers become a drag on your small business finances.

In closing and summing it all up, unconventional wisdom says that "if your customers are big and slow, factoring is the way to go."

Chapter 9 Success Factors

1. Factors screen your customers to determine how credit-worthy they are.

2. True power lies in using your own money, with no debt, through advances made against the accounts receivables from your own sales.

3. If you follow only one piece of advice in this book, let it be this one: **Alternative Financing products like Factoring are the most opportunistic and best methods available to ensure the growth and success of your small-to-medium-sized business.**

Parting Wisdom

Well, we've come to the end. But before we close, I would like to share a few more things with you.

The knowledge, wisdom and insights shared in this book are taken from the collective experience accumulated over more than twenty-five years of doing business in diverse corners of the world, with people from many different backgrounds. The lessons that I've shared differ from the conventional teachings of say, a business school or economics textbook, where situations are predictable, systems perform as planned, and people behave as expected. The world of business, and this is true for both small and large companies, doesn't always follow our script, and as a result, requires a different approach. And that's what this book is about. I'm challenging you to continue to be diligent and make your best-laid plans, but at the same, understand and expect that things will be different and embrace the possibilities that these differences will present.

I truly hope that you have enjoyed the things I've shared with you as much as I've enjoyed writing them. And remember to always have in mind the Success Factors: keep the passion and your dreams alive about your business; stick to your plan and follow your timeline; plan for the unpredictable; have a clear path to making money; give generously; and keep in mind that factoring solutions represent some of the best and quickest ways to finance your business growth, and subsequently, your success. If you think about it, that's not so unconventional after all, is it?

Tchau, tchau

Tchau, tchau (or 'bye bye' in Portuguese) for now, but let me know how it goes. Seriously. Now that we've spent this time together, I feel vested in your success.

Visit me at: **www.successfactormedia.com**, and register for my newsletter: subscribe@successfactormedia.com

Now that we're friends, let's connect:

Facebook: https://www.facebook.com/SuccessFactorMedia/

Twitter: @SuccessFactorMedia

LinkedIn: https://www.linkedin.com/in/ernaneiung/

Appendix A - Rethinking Conventional Wisdom

Conventional wisdom says businesses fail because they run out of cash.

Unconventional wisdom: Businesses don't fail because they lack cash, they lack cash because they have failed.

Conventional wisdom says you can do anything you set your mind to.

Unconventional wisdom: Play to your strengths, using your natural advantages, and quickly seize the opportunity you have identified, because it may not be around for long.

Conventional wisdom says there is a magic formula for success.

Unconventional wisdom: The path to success is unpredictable, so set clear goals, plan for uncertainty, and go the distance.

Conventional wisdom says "timing is everything," suggesting that anyone who comes up with the right idea at the right time can't help but succeed.

Unconventional wisdom: The timeline is everything. Hold onto your starting capital as long as possible. Carefully time your launch expenses and manage your operating cash flow to avoid putting yourself behind the eight ball before you've even banked your first revenue.

Conventional wisdom says, "If you build it, they will come."

Unconventional wisdom: Define your ideal customer. Make their lives better. And do it better than anyone else.

Conventional wisdom says cast a wide net to catch and keep as many customers as possible.

Unconventional wisdom: A few well-chosen customers, with whom you enjoy working, are worth more than many who make your life miserable.

Conventional wisdom says business owners must be well schooled in myriad marketing methods – advertising, telemarketing, direct mail, POS marketing, pipeline development, conversion, satisfaction, and retention, to name a few.

Unconventional wisdom: Marketing, while important, varies by industry, product, and service offerings; but relationships developed and nurtured from focused efforts in referral marketing, are the key drivers and success factors for a small-to-medium sized business and its customers.

Conventional wisdom says, if you want something done right, do it yourself.

Unconventional wisdom: Use *The Success Factor's* "4 Ps of Outsourcing," to tailor a strategy around the strengths & weaknesses of your company, as well as its specific needs.

Conventional wisdom says outbo

und marketing — paid advertising, cold calls, mass emails

to purchased lists, direct mail, and telemarketing — is the best way to prospect for customers.

Unconventional wisdom: You need a digital strategy to attract and pre-qualify leads, and increase conversion rates at much lower acquisition cost than traditional outbound marketing.

Conventional Wisdom says use bank financing to meet all your businesses liquidity needs.

Unconventional Wisdom: Factoring is not an after-thought. Use it from Day 1 of your new business to provide you the working capital and liquidity you need to grow your business to success.

Appendix B – List of Success Factors

1. Make a list of your natural assets/advantages.

2. Determine whether any of those assets will give you an advantage over competitors.

3. Make sure you are putting your natural advantages to their highest and best use.

4. Build your "'bilities."

5. Quantify how much money you'll make, how long you'll wait to get paid, and how you're going to bridge any critical gaps.

6. READY – Focus intensely on your basic start-up goals: i) get operational, ii) start the clock, and iii) control the timeline.

7. AIM – Plan for the unpredictable using a detailed, highly flexible business plan.

8. FIRE – Execute effectively by keeping your goals in mind

and conserving resources to "go the distance."

9. RELOAD - Plan for growth from the get-go.

10. Build a detailed, in-depth timeline as a central piece of the business plan.

11. Go from being a consumer, to a producer, of cash as quickly as you can.

12. Time large initial expenditures as close as possible to your first influx of cash from sales.

13. Take care of the 5 Ps of a perfect timeline: place, permission, payability, product, and people.

14. Ask what problems your proposed product or service solves. Do the research on problem solving before you invest in a product or service offering.

15. Determine what your end users need that you could provide.

16. Differentiate to create a winning value proposition for your product or service.

17. Avoid crowds, and establish your business in a city, municipality, state, or country which provides you and your business a competitive advantage.

18. When the competitive landscape gets too crowded, do like an aquatic marathoner and distance yourself from the crowd; but in business, do it by going upstream.

19. Find the optimal combination of price and quality that makes it impossible for your customer to even consider going to your competitor instead.

20. Consistently review whether the experience of the ultimate user of your product or service could be improved.

21. Always negotiate with awareness that customers are in it for themselves.

22. Know that customers will use suppliers and service providers as leverage to satisfy their end consumers.

23. Don't let your business evolve to overwhelming dependence on one particular customer.

24. Understand the problems your company will solve for the customer.

25. Demonstrate that the cost of NOT solving problems is greater than the cost of solving them.

26. Paint a complete, detailed picture of your ideal customer.

27. Look for customers you enjoy working with, who also have money.

28. Develop a communication strategy that repels the people you don't want to work with, and attracts those you do want to work with.

29. Relationships are the key to obtaining and retaining customers.

30. Define your customer in order to choose your specific market.

31. Unselfishly giving to your referral network is the way to grow your market.

32. Use my 4 Ps of Outsourcing (Planning, Picking, Phasing In/Out, and Partnering) to determine what you should do yourself, and what should be outsourced.

33. Evaluate your processes after launch, and prune those that are not needed to sustain a going concern.

34. Partner with other small businesses to share common overhead, such as administrative staff, communications

systems, office space, and IT infrastructure.

35. A digital strategy, including a mobile-friendly platform and inbound marketing, is absolutely essential if your business is going to survive and thrive.

36. A website should serve as your online headquarters, communications hub, recruiting center, showroom, marketing kiosk, sales floor, customer service department, and vendor portal.

37. Mass marketing and cold-calling have been replaced with targeted and hyper-personal online engagement strategies designed to convert "warm leads" into customers.

38. Factors screen your customers to determine how credit-worthy they are.

39. True power lies in using your own money, with no debt, credit approval requirement, or waiting.

40. If you follow only one piece of advice in this book, let it be this one: **Alternative Financing products like Factoring are the most opportunistic and best methods available to ensure the growth and success of your small-to-medium-sized business.**

Appendix C – Glossary of Terms

(sources: dictionary.com, thesaurus.com, and Wikipedia.com)

TERM	DEFINITION
accounts receivable factoring	expediting cash flow through selling invoices to a factor
advance	money paid ahead of the time it is due
alternative financing	financial channels and instruments emerging outside traditional finance systems such as regulated banks and capital markets
AR	Accounts Receivable - money owed to a company
assets	total resources of a person or business, as cash, notes, accounts receivable, securities, inventories, goodwill, fixtures, machinery, or real estate
avatar	embodiment or personification of a principle, attitude, or view of life
B2B	Business-to-business - commerce transactions between businesses, such as between manufacturer and wholesaler, or between a wholesaler and retailer
back office	systems of secure e-commerce software that process company information, including databases
bad debt	amount owed to a creditor that is unlikely to be paid and which a creditor is not willing to take action to collect
bankruptcy	complete financial depletion

TERM	DEFINITION
bilities test	three concepts that frame a business model: scalability, replicability, and sustainability
blog	website containing a writer's experiences, observations, and opinions
break-even	having income exactly equal to expenditure, thus showing neither profit nor loss
budget	itemized estimate of expected income and expenses for a given time
business model	defines the way you do business
business plan	defines specific goals and objectives
BYO	bring your own
call to action	implicit or explicit suggestion contained in marketing content
CAN - SPAM Act	law that sets compliance rules for commercial email
cash flow	real or virtual movement of money
cash inflow	receipts of money
cash outflow	financial obligations and payments of money
CFO	Chief Financial Officer - head of company finances
click	selection of a screen object on a computer or handheld device by rapidly depressing and releasing a button on a mouse or other input device

TERM	DEFINITION
click-through rate	ratio of users who click on a specific link to the number of total users who view a page, email, or advertisement
close ratio	number of deals closed compared to the number of presentations made
Cloud (the)	type of internet-based computing that provides shared computer processing resources and data to computers and other devices on demand
collateralize	secure a loan with property or securities
contact list	list of acquaintances, colleagues, and relatives, along with ways to get in touch with them, as email addresses, postal addresses, and telephone numbers
conventional wisdom	a generally-accepted theory or belief
conversion rate	percentage of visitors to a website who become customers
corporation	association of individuals, created by law or under authority of law, having a continuous existence independent of its members, and powers and liabilities distinct from those of its members
default rates	interest rate charged by a lender if borrower fails to meet payment obligation

TERM	DEFINITION
deliverability rate	success rate an email marketer has in getting an email delivered to a person's email address; number of emails delivered, divided by number of emails sent
demand generation	focus of targeted marketing programs to drive awareness and interest in a company's products and/or services
differentiation	act or process or state of making different by modification, or perceiving the difference in or between
ebook	book in digital form to be read on a computer or hand-held device as a tablet or smartphone
economies of scale	cost advantages that enterprises obtain due to size, output, or scale of operation, with cost per unit of output generally decreasing with increasing scale, as fixed costs are spread out over more units of output
end-user	ultimate user for whom a machine, as a computer, or product, as a computer program, is designed
entrepreneur	person who organizes and manages any enterprise, especially a business, usually with considerable initiative and risk
entrepreneurial	dealing with an employer of productive labor or a contractor

TERM	DEFINITION
equipment leasing	contractual agreement arranging for the lessee (user) to pay the lessor (owner) for the use of anything kept, furnished, or provided for a specific purpose
ERP	Enterprise Resource Planning - business management software that uses integrated applications to automate back office functions related to technology, human resources, and services
Facebook	online social media and networking service that allows users to create a user profile, add other users as friends, exchange messages, post status updates and digital photos, share digital videos and links, use various software applications, and receive notifications when others update their profiles or make posts
freelance	person who works selling services by the hour, day, job, etc., rather than working on a regular basis for on employer
goodwill	intangible, salable asset arising from the reputation of a business and its relations with its customers, distinct from the value of its stock and other tangible assets
intellectual property	individual product of original creative thought and property that results, as patents, copyright material, and trademarks

TERM	DEFINITION
inventory	detailed, descriptive list of articles, merchandise, or stock on hand, raw materials, finished goods on hand, etc. made periodically by a business concern
invoice	itemized bill for goods sold or services provided, containing individual prices, total charge, and terms
lead generation	marketing process of stimulating and capturing interest in a product or service for the purpose of developing sales pipelines
liability insurance	part of general insurance system of risk financing to protect the purchaser from the risk of liabilities imposed by lawsuits and similar claims
LinkedIn	business and employment-oriented social networking service that operates via websites
liquidity	ability or ease with which assets can be converted to cash
LLC	Limited Liability Corporation - private business structure that combines the pass-through taxation of a partnership or sole proprietorship with the limited liability of a corporation
loading speed	how quickly a website downloads to a device via the internet
metrics	standard for measuring or evaluating something, especially using figures or statistics
minimize the maximum	minimizing cash outflow by moving large expenses toward the end of the start-up phase

TERM	DEFINITION
niche	distinct segment of a market
OEM	Original Equipment Manufacturer - company that makes a part or subsystem that is used in another company's end product
offline	operating independently of, or disconnected from, an associated computer
operating licenses	certificate issued by a government agency allowing an individual or company to provide a controlled type of activity
OSHA	Occupational Safety and Health Administration - federal agency of the United States that regulates workplace safety and health
outsourcing	purchasing goods or subcontracting services from an outside supplier or source
P&L	Profit and Loss statement - one of the financial statements of a company, and shows the company's revenues and expenses during a particular period
portfolio	total holdings of securities, commercial paper, etc. of a financial institution or private investor
procurement	act of obtaining or getting by effort, care, or the use of special means - equipment, materials or supplies

TERM	DEFINITION
profit margin	percentage that the monetary surplus left to a producer or employer (after deducting wages, rent, cost of raw materials and the like) constitutes of total sales
promotional	devised to publicize or advertise a product, cause, institution, etc., as a brochure, free sample, poster, television or radio commercial, or personal appearance
prospects	potential or likely customers or clients
public relations	art, technique, or profession of promoting goodwill of between a corporation, store, government, individual, etc. and the public, community, employees, customers, etc.
purchase order financing	funding option for businesses that need cash to fill single or multiple customer orders
referral culture	state when referrals are incorporated into company culture
replicability	capacity for duplication
retainer	fee paid to secure services
risk mitigation	systematic reduction in the extent of exposure to a risk and/or the likelihood of its occurrence
scalability	ability of something, especially a computer system, to adapt to increased demands

TERM	DEFINITION
segmentation	division into segments
SEO	Search Engine Optimization - process of affecting the visibility of a website or a web page in a web search engine's unpaid results
SKU	Stock Keeping Unit - a retailer-defined coding system used to distinguish individual items within a retailer's accounting, warehousing, and point-of-sale systems
smartphone	device that combines a cell phone with a handheld computer, typically offering internet access, data storage, email capability, etc.
social media	websites and other online means of communication that are used by large groups of people to share information and to develop social and professional contacts
sole proprietorship	business entity that is owned and run by one natural person and in which there is no legal distinction between the owner and the business
spam	disruptive online messages, especially commercial messages posted on a computer network or sent as email
start-up	period of time between beginning the process of putting the physical infrastructure of your company in place, until the moment you issue your first invoice

TERM	DEFINITION
success factor	management term for an element that is critically necessary for an organization or project to achieve its mission
sustainability	whether an operation can maintain its profitability over time
timeline	linear representation of important events in the order in which they occurred; a schedule or timetable
tollgate	passing from one stage of a project to the next in business
transfer of trust	when a referring person expresses trust in a referred person to a referee
tweet	message on Twitter, restricted to 140 characters
Twitter	online news and social networking service where users post and interact with messages called "tweets," restricted to 140 characters
unconventional wisdom	theory or belief not bound by or conforming to rule or procedure; unorthodox
underwriting	to bind oneself to contribute a sum of money to an undertaking, or to assume liability to the extent of a specified sum by way of insurance
virtual	temporarily simulated or extended by computer software
win-win	advantageous to both sides, as in negotiation

TERM	DEFINITION
WMS	Warehouse Management System - software application designed to support warehouse or distribution center management and staff
word-of-mouth	informal oral communication
YouTube	video-sharing website that allows users to upload, view, rate, share, add to favorites, report, and comment on videos

About The Author

The son of a physician and second of three boys, Ernane Iung landed in Flint, Michigan at the age of 7-months. His family planned to return to his native Brazil at the completion of his father's residency program. But, like so many other families, his stayed; and today, Ernane is the product of the combination of a Brazilian upbringing in a Midwestern home.

That upbringing laid the foundation for an executive career spanning 28-years, twenty of which were spent overseas in São Paulo, Brazil where he solidified his career working for multinationals with such household names as GE, Whirlpool, Philips, and Oster. His international career has taken him across four continents, with travels all throughout Brazil and South America, in addition to Canada, China, Holland, Italy, Mexico, Spain, South Africa, and Saudi Arabia, just to name a few. Ernane has been a C-Suite executive for more than 11-years and is an expert at running small companies, having done so with the sales subsidiaries of the multinationals he has lead. As part of this experience he has worked with hundreds of small businesses, ranging from mom & pop stores, corporations, and family businesses to start-ups; and it is this wealth of experience that has created the groundwork for this book.

Today, Ernane is president and owner of Liquid Capital Solutions, located in Orlando, Florida and part of Liquid Capital

Corporation, headquartered in Toronto, Canada. Liquid Capital is one of the industry leaders in alternative financing and has a network of over 85 finance professionals spread across the U.S. and Canada. They offer a full suite of financing products ranging from factoring and purchase order financing, to asset based lending, import/export financing, equipment leasing, and working capital advances.

Ernane is a member of the Hispanic Chamber of Commerce, the Association for Corporate Growth, the Turnaround Management Association, the National Center for Simulation, a Key Person of Influence, and the International Factoring Association. He is an elite competitive swimmer who specializes in aquatic marathons, loves wines and travel, and enjoys cooking for his wife and two daughters at their home in Orlando, Florida.

And now, as *The Success Factor*, Ernane is sharing his years of proven success strategies through his blog and online webinars, in speaking engagements, and here, in this book.

Morgan James
Speakers Group

www.TheMorganJamesSpeakersGroup.com

We connect Morgan James published
authors with live and online events
and audiences whom will benefit
from their expertise.

Morgan James makes all of our titles available through the Library for All Charity Organization.

www.LibraryForAll.org

Printed in the USA
CPSIA information can be obtained
at www.ICGtesting.com
JSHW082340140824
68134JS00020B/1792